Travelling Light

Travelling Light

Agnes Braceland Henchey

Shoreline

Copyright 2004, Agnes Braceland Henchey

Cover and layout by Sarah Robinson
Photographs property of the author

Printed in Canada by AGMV Marquis

Published by Shoreline, 23 Ste-Anne
Ste-Anne-de-Bellevue, Quebec, Canada H9X 1L1
Phone/fax 514-457-5733
shoreline@sympatico.ca   www.shorelinepress.ca

Dépôt legal: National Library of Canada
et la Bibliothèque nationale de Québec

National Library of Canada Cataloguing in Publication

Henchey, Agnes Braceland, 1925-
Travelling light / Agnes (Patty) Braceland Henchey.
ISBN 1-896754-33-3
1. Henchey, Agnes Braceland, 1925- 2. Travel agents—Canada—
Biography. I. Title.
G154.5.H45A3 2004   338.4'791'092   C2004-900215-5

DEDICATION

To the memory of
our parents, Anna Chandler and Vincent Braceland,
who taught us the meaning of love and giving;
our brother Lawrence . S.J.;
and our sister Jean and her husband, Justice Jacques Bertrand.
R.I.P.

To my sisters and brother and their spouses:
Phyllis, R.S.C.J., of Halifax, Nova Scotia,
who just celebrated her ninetieth birthday;
Rita and her husband, Redman, "Red," Langan, of Aurora, Ontario;
Connie and her husband, Bob Degenhart, of Columbia,
South Carolina;
Hugh and his wife, Pat Wood, of Nepean, Ontario.

To
my husband, Gordon Henchey;

our children:
Michael,
Peter and his wife, Diane Sirkin,
Brian and his wife, Lisa Lane,
Elizabeth Ann (Betty Anne) and her husband,
Chris Foote.

our grandchildren:
Emily, Matthew and Patrick Henchey
and Nicole Erin Foote

ACKNOWLEDGEMENTS

My thanks to Timothy Fain, a teacher who also conducts a course in Creative Writing. I chose the Beaconsfield Library venue, although the course is also held in the Pointe Claire Library. Tim encouraged me to keep writing in any style that suited my comfort level. He guided rather than pushed, and I am very grateful to him.

To all the course attendees I have met, I thank you for your support and critiques which were never critical. They were helpful. I wish you luck in all your endeavours, especially your creative ones.

To Judith Isherwood, I offer my thanks for reading my book and of course for publishing. Writing was fun, but when it came to putting it all together, I needed some help, and it was there for me. Thank you, Judith.

To Jane Barclay Pearce, a published author of children's books, whose advice I sought, and who shared information and experiences with me.

Lastly, but most important, I thank my husband, Gordon, whose patience hasn't run out yet, although I don't understand why.

THE HALIFAX EXPLOSION

It was Halifax. It was hell. It was the holocaust without hatred — a devastation without discrimination. It was December 6th, 1917.

A munitions ship, loaded in every nook and cranny with dynamite, arriving to join a convoy, collided with another at the narrows leading into Bedford Basin. A massive explosion occurred — the worst man-made disaster in Canadian history — wreaking death and destruction on the city of Halifax. Two thousand people died instantly, their body parts scattered over the northern section of the city. Others died in prolonged pain. Some recovered physically, but were scarred for life by unimaginable sights and sounds of agony. Some longed for death to end the pain, but were not masters of their own destinies, and lived courageously in quiet desperation, each empathizing with the other without a word being spoken — only the eyes told of sorrow. Today when I visit this beautiful rebuilt city, I marvel at the love that emanates from the people I meet. They have learned something very important, which has been passed down to them from those who lost everything but their spirit on that fateful December day.

At that time, our father was an aspiring reporter for the *Halifax Herald*. He had a young family, a boy and two girls just old enough to be attending kindergarten and grade school. The children had colds and Mum had kept them home from school, but when Dad called and told her to take them to the golf course, she bundled them up and raced away from the house that was in danger of crumbling from the many explosions still taking place. The two girls, Phyllis and Jean, were in the carriage, and the little boy, Lawrence, struggled to keep pace, his feet slipping on the ice and snow.

Every window in the *Halifax Herald* offices was shattered inward, and there were many deaths and serious injuries. Dad did what he could for his confrères and then joined a rescue group to enter houses, those still standing and those which had been hit. He made sure that the occupants left the dwellings and headed to relative safety. Some of the elderly had to be carried out and left until rescue trucks and other vehicles passed by to pick up the stranded.

Dad entered a damaged house. He called out to see if anyone was there and a frail voice answered, "I'm upstairs." The steps of the stairs that had been hit were now a pile of debris on the floor. A few steps were hanging down, and it would be a big job to get to his destination. Very gingerly, he supported himself on whatever he found to be somewhat solid, and with great care and difficulty, was able to hoist himself up to the second floor. He searched the rooms and found a very old woman propped up in a single bed. He told her what had happened and said he would take good care of her. In the later telling of his story, he always said he had no idea how he would carry her down that partly blown-out staircase, but the thought that she was someone's mother gave him the courage to try. She was as light as a feather, and on closer scrutiny, had to be at least ninety years old. At the top of the stairwell he faced the biggest challenge of his young life. How could he possibly save her and himself? It would be difficult enough to manage the few steps alone. And there his story ends.

It resumes as he places her on a large rock in front of the house and warns her not to move, for a rescue vehicle will be along very soon. With a sad but mischievous, toothless smile the woman answers, "Now, just a minute, young fella me boy, I haven't been outta that bejasus house in twenty years, and I ain't never going back. You understand, laddie?" Of all the rescues our father made, this one stood out in his memory as a bit of humour in a hellhole of horror, as a ray of hope in a world of hopelessness that was Halifax that day.

MEMORIES

In 3431 Rosedale Avenue in Montreal, Quebec, Canada, two very remarkable people, our parents, had a great deal of influence not only upon the lives of their children, but upon the many people whom they knew. As a daughter of Anna Chandler Braceland and Vincent Braceland, there is no doubt in my mind that they taught me more than right from wrong. My admiration for them is boundless. As parents, they did not preach The Way, but showed The Way, and I am eternally grateful. I am confident that each one of us in the Braceland family took away from Rosedale Avenue a sense of family love, bonds of fidelity, pride in each other, empathy in sorrow, and joy in happiness.

So Rosedale Avenue was the scene of our childhood, at least for me, as I was only one year old when we moved there from St. Lambert. I am a part of the Braceland Family, a part of the four-bedroom home that housed our parents and my siblings and me, and that holds so many wonderful memories and, I would suspect, some intriguing secrets. Each time I am in the vicinity of Rosedale, I park the car at 3431 and let my imagination bring back to me the sights and sounds that are so precious.

I happened to be the youngest, coming after Lawrence, Phyllis, Jean, Rita, Hughie and Connie. Being the youngest and smallest had its advantages, which I was to learn very early on. Being the lightest, I was less of a burden when I climbed up on our father's knee to stroke and tousle his fine head of thick chestnut-coloured hair. At the end of a long day, I suppose he welcomed this distraction. It did not occur to me that each and every one of my siblings had already been through this stage, so I considered it a unique experience. At dinnertime, I sat next to Dad and whispered my important news exclusively to him. On looking back, my siblings must have frowned on this display, for it was attention I hardly deserved. I did enjoy getting out of as much work as possible. When I was old enough, around five or six, I would meet Dad at the streetcar stop about two blocks away, take his hand and walk him home. How proud I was, for even then I sensed his respectability and stature in the community. He always presumed that I had been overworked at home during the day and it was my pleasure to agree, and even embellish my accomplishments.

My first recollection of 3431 is when I was about four years old. I pinpoint the time because my brother Lawrence was still at home, and he didn't leave for the Jesuit seminary until 1929. Dad and Lawrence were in a teasing mood, and would go into gales of laughter as they told me to search for a big bee that was just behind me. As I did, they swiped my little doll carriage. Looking back I see them acting like five-year-old boys, but then it was enraging. I remember howling and roaring, and the more I did the more they laughed. It must have been an irresistibly funny sight for them in their childish mood, but I was not amused. I do believe that was the start of my bad temper, which took me years to control. That, however, was the one and only time an event of this nature happened. I often think it is too bad it is my first recollection of my brother Lawrence, whom I saw again only years later when he came to Montreal for more training as a Jesuit. He was the kindest, most thoughtful man and I was proud to have him as an older brother.

Our home had a centre hall plan. On entering, there was a good-sized vestibule (we call it "porch" now), then a large hall with a wide arch on the right to the living room that ran the full depth of the house. On the other side was a lovely dining room, a fairly big kitchen and a pantry where Mum kept her canned goods. At the back of this pantry was a step-up to two doors behind which were housed ice blocks which kept the milk and butter cold. As a small child, I envisioned all kinds of weird and scary things waiting to bite my hand off as I reached in for a quart of milk. But then, I always imagined the despicable creatures who awaited me in the basement and would bite off my legs as I flew up the stairs, clutching a jar of preserves that Mum had asked me to take to her from the cold storage.

In those days, I was a very fussy and light eater. Food was something I had to endure. That has all changed. Now, if I'm not hungry, please call an ambulance and check my pulse, for I am probably dead. In those days, we ate lunch in the kitchen, and Mum would try to entice me to eat. A crying match would ensue and in desperation Mum would threaten to put me in the pantry. (It was a rather large room with a window, and not a threatening experience for most people). To my recollection, I spent quite some time in the pantry kicking and hollering, simply because I was too stubborn to give in. I was terrified of the two doors, and knew something was going to grab me, but still I would not comply, nor would I tell Mum I was afraid. How hard I made life for myself, and what about my dear mother, who must have wanted to strangle me, but her gentleness prevented her from doing so.

I have always thought that three is a bad number, with respect to groups of people. I had a good friend, Betty Savidant, who lived next door. She is now in Akron, Ohio, and we still keep in touch. We would play together amicably until sister Connie would show up. Betty would immediately abandon me and succumb to Connie's charms. They would run off together to undisclosed places and treasures. My consolation was to have a chat with Jesus, and tell Him that I really didn't care, because when I got to Heaven, I would know where they went. I wasn't quite sure where Heaven was, but Mum always made it sound safe and secure. Perhaps my longing for peace in Heaven gave me the notion that becoming a nun might secure my passage to this Haven (to spite Connie, no doubt). I was later to be discouraged in my halfhearted pursuit of this life when a friend advised me that if I became a nun, as a test of my obedience, my Superior would probably tell me to scrub the stairs by starting at the bottom. Well, scrubbing the stairs wasn't exactly my idea of the Sisterhood, especially if I would have to accept a dumb order like that. So, another insight took place — obedience was not to be my forte.

THE CASKET

In was springtime, I was seven, and we had just been blessed with the arrival of a sweet little baby boy, to add to the brood now living in the house on Rosedale Avenue. That made eight, and my position as the youngest was lost forever. He was the darling of the house, having a sunny disposition, the face of an angel and a head of beautiful blond curls. Terry's beauty and personality would touch the hardest of hearts. As our little brother grew, he replaced me on our father's knee, joined Dad on little walks around the neighbourhood and tousled Dad's hair. As I look back, I recall no jealousy, for this baby with the huge blue eyes was the most lovable child. When he learned to talk, the men of the family taught him to say, "He shoots, he scores," to the delight of all.

When Terry was seventeen months old, Dad took the rest of us on a trip to see some favourite relatives in Detroit. Mum stayed home with Terry and my two oldest sisters. We travelled by train, as Dad worked for the Canadian National Railways in their public relations department, promoting their services to the American travel industry. We dined in the parlour car, and considered that this was probably the best invention since butterscotch. We were a well-behaved group, for our father did not tolerate any misbehaviour, especially where *his* railroad was concerned. The trip went very well from our point of view, and even my brother Hughie was not up to much mischief. He was having too much fun counting telephone poles and, when he got to a random number, seeing how many times he could divide it by seven or nine. It exasperated us girls, who were planning what wonderful events would take place in Detroit. In all fairness to Hughie, he did have a mathematical bent, and would be the first Canadian to graduate from Parkes Air College at the University of St. Louis, as an aeronautical engineer. This was just after the war and aeronautical engineering was not a part of Canadian university studies.

13

One day before our planned week was over, Aunt Gertrude answered the telephone and said to Dad, "It's for you, Vince. It's Annie. I think it's serious." The news was that our baby was sick. The family doctor had declared it a teething problem, but Mum had had enough experience to recognize a teething problem from a serious illness. Dad told her to call Dr. Goldbloom, a specialist, then call back with the results. It *was* serious, for in those days we did not use long-distance telephone except in emergencies. Mum telephoned later to say that Dr. Goldbloom had come to the house and had said to burn all Terry's toys — he thought our little brother had spinal meningitis. Our holiday was over, and our trip home a sombre one, Hughie counting the telephone poles silently this time.

Terry was in the Children's Hospital when we returned, and Dr. Goldbloom said we should pray that God would take our baby, for if he lived, he would be like a vegetable. God did make the decision to call Terry, and he died a few days later. My oldest brother, Lawrence, wrote a wonderful poem, the first verses of which are

O child of Grace, O little One,
You came from God's own hand.
Why He in haste reclaimed you soon
We scarce can understand.

Wise in His eternity
An angel child He made
With beauty winged and brilliancy
That seemed could never fade.

The last lines are about accepting the will of God. In those days, it was the practice to hold the wake at home. The undertakers brought Terry home in a little white coffin, and put it on a white device that looked like an accordian. Our telephone rang constantly, and the doorbell also, from early in the day to late in the evening. Our neighbours brought wonderful casseroles, cakes, pies, cooked ham, roasts, lots of cookies, and homemade bread, for they knew we were a hungry lot. Even in sorrow we children never skipped a meal.

The morning of the funeral, I felt especially sad, and did not rise with the others. I stayed in my room a little longer, cherishing sweet bygone memories and trying to accommodate my thinking to the fact that my darling Terry would not be coming to wake me up, and the fact that I would never again see him after today. An idea was slow in forming, but I made up my mind. I would carry it through.

The family were in the kitchen, having a second cup of tea, bracing themselves for the day to come. I crept down the stairs and gingerly slid around the opening to the living room. I approached Terry, kissing his little face. Ice met my lips and my body quivered with the coldness of the touch. What had happened? It was summer still, and our home was warm and humid. I was frightened, but nonetheless the job had to be done. I leaned over to my brother's head and placed my scissors on one gold ringlet. Hastily I slashed that curl, and placed it in my hand, still shaking with the fright of the cold, and the devious deed I was doing. At that moment, the casket cover slammed down on my thumb, causing me to breath deeply so that I would not scream. I dropped the curl and the scissors, my only thought being to escape this nightmare, this deed of the devil, or perhaps it was God's wrath for my misdeed. I wondered if there was blood on the white satin, but I had no time to think about it. Get out! Get upstairs before you are discovered, my mind told my legs, as I went scampering up the stairs to the landing, where I hid, waiting for the discovery by my family.

I heard chairs scraping the kitchen floor, feet moving quickly into the living room, and then I heard our father say, "It's hard to believe the casket cover could make such a terrible noise. I'll have to make a couple of wedges so it can't happen again." Then it was my eighteen-year-old sister saying, "Mum, look what I found on the floor — a lock of Terry's hair. How could that have happened?" My mother remained calm for a moment or two and said slowly, "I snipped a lock of Terry's hair. When the doorbell rang, I must have dropped it." My sister said, "And why were you using the butter cutter scissors?" Slowly, surely, Mum answered, "Because I didn't want to put anything sharp near our baby's head." Oh, Mum, how I love you. You understand everything. Even in your great sorrow you are protecting me and would do so for each one of us. You know my oldest sister is somewhat of a thorn in my side, don't you?

I continued up the stairs, now out of danger. A few moments later, I recognized Mum's step on the staircase. She entered the room, sat down on the bed, and said, "I know you are very sad today. We all are. I know that's why you didn't come down for breakfast. Now get dressed, come downstairs, and I'll fix a special breakfast just for you."

Oh, Mum, how I love you. You are kindness in chaos, you are sweet where there is no sweetness, you are wise where there seems to be no wisdom.

Mum bore this second death — she had lost John Paul at eight days old — with her usual fortitude and devotion to Dad and the rest of the family, mantling her grief with soft smiles and reassurances. Our sister Rita had been Terry's second mother, and I believe she felt the loss even more than we did.

Up until the death of my brother, our father had entertained us daily, playing the piano and singing. He was very gifted, and if we came home with a new tune, we simply sang it for him and away he went, playing it beautifully. After Terry died, the house was silent, and I longed for Dad to belt out "Won't You come Home, Bill Bailey?" or "Betty Coed" or "When Irish Eyes are Smiling." He used to play and sing a favourite of mine "Two Little Girls in Blue, Lad," but I have never heard that song again. It was many years before Dad's grief yielded to acceptance, and I think he suffered more than we could comprehend. We watched his hair turn a snowy white almost overnight. I never knew how Mum coped with her losses. She never spoke of them, but her deep faith was the most important factor.

THE AMATEUR HOUR

When I was in third grade, our school was closed and moved into a brand new, ultra modern building. Quite a radical change from the two-story house on Belmore Avenue that had also served my older sisters and brothers. I remember before I was six, sometimes one of my siblings would take me to class if Mum was ill, which didn't seem to happen very often. These were thrilling experiences, even though sometimes, depending on the sister I was accompanying, the classes were held in the basement, with only a sand floor. I had been told that they had seen mice in that basement, so at first I was quite hesitant to accompany my sisters. However, the day came when I myself spotted a mouse running between the desks, and was quick to join the other students when they jumped up on their desks, squealing as only girls can at the sight of an unwanted varmint. I attended this school at the age of six, but my classes were never in that dreaded basement. That building still stands, and has been upgraded, sold and resold many times in the seventy-odd years since I called it my grade school.

Along with the new school, came a new principal, Mr. Shaw, not to be confused with Mrs. Shaw who taught at the old school, and whom we thought was married to the new man. Mrs. Shaw was feared and loved by all of my siblings, who even now talk about her devotion to learning. She had white hair, but I can't now remember her facial features. I do however recall that her black dresses always kissed her black laced walking shoes. I never think of Mrs. Shaw without remembering the long pointer she carried, although I do believe there were moments when she was without it. She was slightly bent over, no doubt caused by carrying the burden of the likes of us. Mr. Shaw, on the other hand, was a gray-haired, trim gentleman, who walked smartly with a soldierly gait and sported a broad smile — no, it was more like a grin — when he saw or heard something amusing. I imagine we children did come up with some outlandish stories he had heard many times before, but which still tickled his fancy. After about a month with us, he knew every child by name (a feat, even though there were only about twelve students in each class.)

He often stopped to chat a moment if we passed him in the hall. His silver hair, combed straight back, contributed a certain sternness that belied his little grin. We agreed that, like our father, he commanded respect without having to ask for it, and while Mr. Shaw was very friendly, we knew that anyone crossing a little invisible line would be taught where the line was, and never wish to cross it again. I believe he had a strap in his office, but I never heard of anyone who had received it at the hands of Mr. Shaw. Looking back, I wonder how we could have thought Mr. and Mrs. Shaw were husband and wife. She was at least twenty years his senior, and looked much older than that. At the age of nine, these facts were not apparent to me, but I remember being somewhat relieved when I found out that old Mrs. Shaw was on her own, and didn't belong to Mr. Shaw, for I felt he deserved better.

Our new school had an auditorium, and Mr. Shaw decided to put it to good use by having an amateur hour. Any child could apply to perform and, fearing there would be too many applicants, I applied the first day, not knowing what I would do — I didn't feel I had any special talent, except for mathematics and English. I spoke to my teacher about it, and Miss Grace Dibenga suggested that I sing, although she had never heard me in action. I went home, and discussed this with my sister Jean, who was eighteen at the time. She knew all the scores from Broadway shows and every word of every popular opera. Dad and Jean would listen to the New York Metropolitan Opera on the radio from New York every Saturday afternoon, and sometimes I joined them. Jean played the piano and sang very well and had lots of boyfriends. I considered her my mentor for this project.

The latest popular song was "Cheek to Cheek," from the movie with Ginger Rogers and Fred Astaire. I thought I could give a fine rendition of this song and would undoubtedly win first prize. All applications were screened by Miss DiBenga, who, upon hearing my choice, was aghast and very diplomatically suggested that I ask Jean, whom she knew, to come up with a more suitable, less risque, number. As far as I was concerned there was no song more suitable than "Cheek to Cheek," for I already knew by heart the melody and lyrics. I had decided I would not dance like Ginger, for it might detract from my rendition of the song.

Jean said she would give some thought to the suggestion of my teacher, and I had to wait one full agonizing day and night for her to come up with a substitute — nothing as romantic as "Cheek to Cheek," but nevertheless acceptable — "Burlington Bertie." This was hardly a classical piece but I would have to do gestures as well as sing, which would definitely ensure my first place in the contest. This is the last of many verses:

> I'm Burlington Bertie, I rise at ten thirty
> And Buckingham Palace I view.
> I stand in the yard while they're changing the guard
> And the Queen shouts across, "Toodle-oo!"
> The Prince of Wales' brother along with some other
> Slaps me on the back and says "Come and see Mother."
> But I'm Bert, Bert, and royalty's hurt.

When they ask me to dine I say no.
I've just had a banana with Lady Diana
I'm Burlington Bertie from Bow.

The more I practiced the more I liked the piece. The more I strutted before Mum's full-length mirror, the more my confidence grew, and my gestures became wilder and funnier. To rehearse, Dad accompanied me on the piano, and I knew for sure I would be a big hit in show business.

I was ready and set to go more than a month before the big day. My anticipation grew in proportion to my confidence, which was growing by leaps and bounds every day.

The eventful moment arrived. I dressed in pants, a white shirt with a black bow tie and Dad's top hat stuffed with tissue paper so it would not fall down and hide my expressive eyes, which were part of the act. I learned on that day that I was the only entry from my class, and was disappointed that the competition would be such an easy one. Onto the stage I pranced, and began my song. It went swimmingly well and I had no stage fright. My performance seemed to be a crowd pleaser and I swelled with pride as I took my final bow, head low, right hand placed over my waist. I was home.

There were no prizes, but the winners were announced by Mr. Shaw. To my amazement a scoundrel by the name of Jack O'Neill, the older brother of my friend Barbara, won hands down with his rendition of "Rose of Tralee." To be perfectly honest, I had feared his performance might, just might, outrank mine, for he looked like an angel, and had a voice to match. He stood perfectly still, made no gestures, his clear sweet voice blending with the soft melody and lyrics of the song. Its beauty broke my heart, and although I did not allow the lurking suspicion of failure to remain with me, in my heart I knew that Jack should be the winner.

After the concert, Mr. Shaw approached me and asked if I had thought of asking for an accompanist. To tell the truth, I had not even considered such a thing — in fact, I didn't know it was possible to be accompanied. In my confident way, I alone was responsible for producing a hit number. No doubt I was quite off key, and the applause had been for my fearless act and being able to get on stage before a full house, with nothing but a gutsy attitude. Nonetheless, I was disappointed with my second place, and vowed to work harder the next time, not realizing that talent had something to do with success.

Fortunately, or unfortunately, depending on whether or not you were part of the audience, I never performed again, for we were not blessed with another amateur hour. It was years before I realized that if I had any talent it was not in show business.

As for Jack O'Neill, he has always remained a friend. It was with great pride that I learned he had been awarded the Order of Canada at the end of last year. I still correspond with his sister Barbara and enjoy hearing about Jack and his family. I wonder if he sang to them as babies. His Order of Canada was not for his singing ability, but in the area of social work with which he is involved in Alberta.

CONNIE

My sister Connie and I were two years apart, and we started to go our separate ways. She had one set of friends, and I another. When I was in the first year of high school, I confided in Connie that my teacher (Miss Bolger) was humiliating me every day by insisting that I go to the blackboard and draw parts of flowers. Obedience was not a quality anyone had noticed in me, but art was a disaster. Every day it continued, with the class joining in her glee, until I seriously considered murder or suicide. I wasn't sure Connie would be empathetic, as she was a model student and well liked by all of her teachers. However, not only did she understand, but she had the problem fixed in record time. I was moved to another class and did very well.

Another incident I recall is the evening I received a telephone call from a Loyola boy, inviting me to his Junior Prom. I accepted with pleasure, not daring to show how excited I was. This was a milestone in my life. The next evening the boy called back and explained that it was really Connie he wanted, but had the names mixed up. Connie came through with flying colours, refusing the date. It was then I knew she had *class,* something she has never lost.

MRS. JESSMER

At age eleven, the world seemed to open up to me, and I felt the urge to explore and look for adventure. Beginning to feel grownup, but clinging to my childlike body and spirit, the latter often won out, and I recall some adventures that today do not make me proud.

I remember Mrs. Jessmer as if it were yesterday. She was probably just a dear old lady, but I did not see her in that light when she made it clear that we (the lot of us who lived on Rosedale Avenue) must not put a foot on her lawn, and Heaven forbid if the can in our game of "Kick the Can" should, by a stroke of misfortune, land on her property. With these instructions, it became increasingly tempting, in fact delectably so, to point the culprit can in the direction of 3437 Rosedale avenue, straight to the heart of Mrs. Jessmer's beautifully manicured lawn. The "kicker" would give that can one rollicking boot and we would all head for the hills, awaiting the wrath of Mrs. Jessmer. She could not see us, but she knew every name in the bunch, and she would call out each name, threatening to call our parents. We, with our cohorts, enjoyed this sport tremendously, and managed to anger Mrs. Jessmer almost every evening.

Another adventure was to await Mrs. Jessmer's arrival as she passed our house on the way home from grocery shopping, her arms laden with the day's purchases. Our favourite trick was to put as much bubble gum into our mouths as was possible without choking. Gum was forbidden by my parents, who considered it unladylike. Therefore this adventure had great appeal for me. As Mrs. Jessmer approached, we would jump out from the hedge, blow huge bubbles until they formed triangles, and huge holes formed in the centers. At this point we would sing very loudly, "Mrs. Jessmer's pants." I can hardly imagine us doing this terrible deed, considering that I thought of myself as a "good child." How charming we must have appeared to this poor old lady, and not once did she report us to our parents, a fact I didn't quite appreciate at the time, for my childish nature did not comprehend the true nature of Mrs. Jessmer. At eleven, my horizons included only my best friends.

Mrs. Jessmer's sudden death would widen my horizons and teach me the meaning of *mea culpa*. When she died, I decided that I wanted to see her to tell her how sorry I was for being so mean. My friend Betty MacDonnell agreed to come with me. We boarded a Number 3 streetcar and travelled downtown to Mountain Street to Wray's Funeral Home.

Before we entered this frightening establishment, I told Betty to let me do the talking. (Why should that be a surprise?) The tall, solemn gentleman with oily, slicked back, grey hair who greeted us wore a black suit with a black bow tie, both matching his expression of doom. He was somewhat stooped, but bent down further to our level as he asked, "And whooooom are you for?" I said, "We would like to see Mrs. Jessmer, please." "Right this way, then." We followed the old bent gentleman, and in doing so, I was composing my speech to Mrs. Jessmer. She might even forgive me, and perhaps would be pouring tea, as Mum did in the living room. I decided then and there that I would eat nothing (not even a cucumber sandwich or a coveted brownie) if offered, as a penance for my behaviour to dear old Mrs. Jessmer. In death, Mrs. Jessmer had become "*Dear* old Mrs. Jessmer" to us.

We entered a very large room, with heavy brocaded drapes drawn over several windows — perhaps so that the sun would not prove a distraction from grief. An antique loveseat on one side of the room and a sad brown chesterfield on the other were both empty. Between two of the windows there was a large brown box. Half of the lid was closed and covered with a spray of white lilies and a crucifix. The old gentleman led me straight to the end of the box where the lid was open, then made a left turn to exit the room. I was staring into the closed eyes of someone or something I did not recognize. Fear clutched at my heart, and I called to Betty to head for the hills. As I turned to make my escape, I all but knocked her down. We fled Wray's Funeral Home, racing up Mountain Street, past Dorchester, over Ste. Catherine, missing our streetcar stop, and stopping only on reaching the safe haven of Sherbrooke Street. We finally stopped to look if the ghost of the funeral parlour was closing in on us. It took some time for us to realize we were safe, and could return to Ste. Catherine Street and the succour of the Number 3 streetcar, heading west.

To this day, I regret having treated Mrs. Jessmer so poorly. In the silence of my heart, however I do remember how much fun we had, the hilarious fits of laughter we enjoyed as we skipped through the adventure of youth, hardly knowing or caring how insensitive we were. I do believe, however, that Mrs. Jessmer knew what it was all about, and perhaps secretly smiled at our idiocy. I have to believe that, Mrs. Jessmer.

22

JEFF HESSLER

Jeff Hessler — Jeff Hessler — I wanted to write a song about this Adonis, but the only word I knew to rhyme was "wrestler," and that word did not fill the bill for a romantic ballad. Ah, yes — Jeff Hessler. My friend Betty MacDonnell and I were secretly in love with him. He was fifteen, Betty was seventeen and I was eleven. We watched him as he rode his bike along our street, but I didn't know the colour of his eyes, for I never did see him face to face, only sideways as he roared by us like the wind, never acknowledging the gawky stares of two love-stricken ugly ducklings.

During the summer holidays, Betty informed me that she had heard that Jeff's two maiden aunts were taking him by ship to England. Somehow Betty found out the date and time of sailing and the name of the ship, which was the *Empress of Canada*. We decided it would be a nice gesture to see Jeff off, and offer him our Bon Voyages wishes. Betty prevailed upon her father to drive us to the docks for this important embarkation. We boarded the ship, and were asked whom we were visiting, since we were not in possession of embarkation passes. We informed the starched uniform that we were with the Hessler Party. Well, the Hessler Party was having a going-away champagne bash with many of the friends of the two Misses Hessler. The party was in one of the private dining rooms, well decorated for the occasion with balloons in every conceivable location. We were ushered into the room, dressed in our finest little togs, and greeted by one Miss Hessler who had no idea who these little kids were. (Betty was a tiny mite who could have been of my vintage.) Both Hessler ladies were very gracious when we informed them that we had come to say *au revoir* to Jeff, and to wish him a fine holiday. When Jeff didn't recognize us — he had never even seen us before, as all our admiration had been done from afar — the Misses Hessler quickly got the picture, and treated us royally, all the while graciously steering us away from their beet-red nephew. Years later, one Miss Hessler walked into my office to book a trip to England (no doubt inspired by the *Empress of Canada*) and I asked her if she remembered the two waifs who had boarded the ship to bid *adieu* so long ago. How well she remembered, and we shared a grin over the episode. She commented that at that very moment, she realized that her little nephew was growing up, and that soon she would be losing him to an adult version of the little girls she met that summer, aboard the beautiful *Empress.*

To this day, I have never uttered a word to Jeff Hessler, nor have I inquired about his life, as I believe this would spoil an illusion. It would be devastating to learn that he was in the hospital suffering from the gout. No, Jeff Hessler remains in my memory just as he was, and there he will stay, for it is pleasant to look back on someone or something deemed perfect, freezing the image, and freeing it from the ravages of time.

WIDER HORIZONS

Up until the age of eleven, my world seemed to be centred around my family, neighbourhood and school friends. However, at eleven, my horizons widened somewhat and I began to notice more happenings in a wider circle. I think it is called growing up.

My school friend Estelle Pouliot invited me to her home, and there I met her mother, who was so different from my own. Mrs. Pouliot was a small, slender woman. She had jet-black hair, an ivory complexion and wore makeup. I was enthralled with her, and could not take my eyes off her manicured nails, lacquered in a bright cherry hue. Her long fingers carefully and artfully held a slim black cigarette holder, and when she inhaled, her nostrils seemed to sing a little song. Dark brown eyes looked straight ahead at me and seemed to be enjoying my fascination. I was invited back several times, and each time I counted the hours until I would again see this beautiful young woman with the cigarette holder. I welcomed the fact that she seemed to have no housework to do, no darning in a basket, and could spare time to pass the day with Estelle and me.

About this time, our parents gave us a nickel once a week for spending money. We would stop at Pete's handy store on our way to school, and buy our favourite treat — honeymoon candies, two for a penny. They were oval, chewy, caramel tooth-breakers, covered in a fine spray of chocolate, and we usually devoured our share in one day. After meeting Mrs. Pouliot, I abandoned the candies and changed my purchase to five Turret cigarettes, five for a nickel. The first time I

24

bought them, I wondered where I would be able to smoke them, for I knew if I was caught, my newfound social life would be drastically curbed. I had to find a safe haven in which to practice my craft. Walking home from school, I would pass the church, and decided that would be a fine spot to practice my newfound pastime. At three-thirty on a weekday, it would surely be empty. It was, and I was to spend many a Turret moment inside. I would twirl the cigarette around, pretending it was in a black holder, and try to hold my fingers as Mrs. Pouliot did, talking to myself as she had talked to me.

I batted my nonexistent eyelashes and answered my own questions, looking straight ahead at a statue of St. Joseph, excusing myself for using him as a prop. Many an exciting moment was spent being Mrs. Pouliot, until my sister Connie, suspecting I was up to no good, popped into the church one afternoon after school, and goodbye Turret Cigarettes. I was to have no nickel for some time, and my spare time would be put to good use with chores designed for a person of my limited moral capacity. My chores would be supervised by my older sister, Connie, who was perfection itself. She explained to me at every opportunity the importance of being trustworthy, a quality I lacked.

While this adventure was taking place, I was not aware that my older brother Hughie had already discovered the art of smoking. His nickel was sometimes withheld from him for one misdemeanour or another. When he found out that I had been discovered smoking, he very graciously offered to show me how to smoke when there were no Turret cigarettes available. I thought he was the smartest person in the world, and so generous to share his talents. Hughie took yesterday's *Star*, lifted out two pages, spread tea leaves in the centre and rolled up the paper tightly into a long cylinder. He explained that when lighting it, one must be sure the tea leaves are in the right position so the match would not hit *only* paper, for that would be dangerous. We practiced this great new trick for quite a few weeks, enjoying ourselves in the privacy of the space under our back gallery. I hated smoking tea leaves, but not wishing to spoil this new relationship with my older brother, didn't share this sentiment with him.

I shared all new secrets with my friend Barbara O'Neill — whose brother had won the amateur-hour contest — and of course this secret was priceless. Except that I had not been a very good pupil of my brother, and was to regret it. One summer afternoon, Barbara's mother was outside hanging laundry, and Barbara thought it would be an opportune time to light up a smoke. She chose the dining room for her experiment, rolled up an empty newspaper and applied an E.B. Eddy match. I had forgotten to tell her about the tea leaves. The paper exploded in flames, and she stuffed it down the radiator cover, which was in front of the window. The curtains went up in flames, and the fire spread rapidly through the house. Three of the five children stayed with us during the rebuilding process of the O'Neill home.

The cause of the fire was not discovered, and it was many years later that Barbara told her family the true story, although she had confided in me immediately after the disaster. I never smoked tea leaves again. My guilt stayed with me for some time. I was truly untrustworthy. Throughout my lifetime, I have had many moments when I have said, "If only I had.... " Yes, if only I had remembered to tell Barbara about the necessity of the tea leaves in her "cigarette."

I lost my fascination with Mrs. Pouliot and Turret cigarettes and gladly returned to my childlike persona, again appreciating the tug and pull of the honeymoon candy so favoured before my smoking interlude. I practiced being trustworthy, but shared this secret with no one.

MORE MEMORIES

Hughie shared another wonderful secret with me. If cold roast beef was not available we could improvise by making pepper sandwiches which he convinced me tasted exactly like roast beef. To this day I still believe it. Hughie had a lovely disposition, and in my younger years before I turned eleven and was still in my whiney stage (which lasted a long time), Mum often assigned jobs to pairs of workers. She pawned me off on Hughie, knowing he would be able to handle me because he never became confrontational with me, which would probably have sent me into a rage. He was as smooth as silk in arranging to keep me occupied without hurting my feelings. One time, our assignment was to polish the wonderful hardwood floors. Hughie sent me on a special mission to find elbow grease, and kept me busy and (I thought) useful. How smart you were, Mum.

26

In those days, before penicillin, "pneumonia" was a dreaded word. Our beloved Hughie contracted this disease, and was very ill. Mum and the doctor used the word "crisis" a lot: if this crisis did not occur, we would lose him. I didn't understand the word, and so thought Jesus might put in an appearance either to take Hughie or to save him. We all prayed very hard, and the crisis did come, Hughie's temperature dropped and he was with us again. What joy in thanksgiving!

With so many girls in the family, I think our father enjoyed the mistaken notion that we were almost perfect. Having experienced the life of a boy, and having been a rather mischievous one himself, he almost always expected Hughie to be the instigator of all mischief. In my experience, that was far from the truth. I don't think my parents wanted to punish any of us, but Dad didn't feel quite so sad if it was a boy rather than a girl. If we girls didn't admit to being the culprit when we were questioned, then it was presumed that we were telling the truth. Not so with Hughie, who would be presumed guilty under almost any circumstances. Hughie never once complained and I often wonder what he thought about in those days when Dad was somewhat hard on him.

At eleven, my horizons broadened to include my sister Rita. I wanted her to be the very best student in her school and offered to help her to cram for her exams. I do believe this was the first time I had thought of a person other than myself. Studying was an obsession, and we would get up very early in the morning in order to go over and over her material. I credited myself with helping her to be first, but if the truth were known, I asked and she answered — over and over again — all of the questions to which she already knew the answers.

When Rita was working, she naturally had some very nice clothes. She didn't buy many things, but had such good taste. The clothes she had were outstanding and she always looked gorgeous. On some winter mornings, I would meet my friend Barbara O'Neill at church. I would be wearing Rita's new bottle-green coat, with a very beautiful black fur collar. She was about three sizes smaller than I, but I was sure I looked very fetching marching up the aisle at the Boarder's Mass — for those young men who were boarders at Loyola. Indeed, age eleven wrought many changes. I helped myself to Rita's coat because I knew I would be back from Mass before she could discover its absence, or mine. It is amazing to me that I didn't feel that sick feeling of guilt, perhaps because I was never caught.

Mum always said that the Father was the Head of the Home and the Mother was the Heart. It was certainly true in our home. After the Stock Market Crash in 1929, when I was four, the Great Depression began. Mum told us repeatedly that there were "men with degrees walking the streets." I watched for them on our street but never saw a man carrying what Mum described. I did see many unfortunates, however, as they lined up at our door awaiting Mum's generosity. She had a reputation for never turning anyone away. These people were looking for money to take home, but would never refuse the meal that Mum provided. If they were not hungry at the moment, she would pack a lunch. Dad repeatedly told her that she should not open the door to these men when she was alone, that she could be murdered. Mum would say that what she gave to the least of these, she gave to God. Dad could not win against this argument. Two generations, almost seventy years later, can any one of us say that we would be so foolhardy as to open the door to any stranger? What a sweet innocent world we found in which to grow up, and which we introduced to our children. When did things go so terribly wrong? What can our grandchildren and great-grandchildren contribute to the improvements needed in the present society?

Our family had a butter-and-egg man whose name was Mr. Stewart. He was a long, thin, stooped gentleman with a brown wrinkled face. He always wore a fedora on his head to protect him from the sun or to hide his bald head. Dad called him Old Stewart (not in his presence) but we were always very polite children, so he was Mr. Stewart to us. On Saturdays he delivered to our back door all the makings for wonderful breakfasts. We had fresh eggs, many pounds of butter, and heavy cream during the berry season. I presumed that Mr. Stewart came straight from his farm to us, and I never did want to find out if this was true, for fear of spoiling an illusion. I think Mr. Stewart secretly admired Mum, not only because she was his best customer, but for her ability to handle a bunch like us.

INNOCENT DECEPTION

June 21st — the first day of our long-awaited summer, and we all piled out of school full of the joy of two months without homework and lots of free time to enjoy the warm weather, the swings at the park, needlework courses, reading books, and whatever else came along.

My sister Connie, who was two years older than I, had just acquired a new boyfriend, Frank McGrath, and of course her time would not be available to me. Bonfires on Tuesday evenings would be spent with him, and I would have to find some other girls who enjoyed singing around the bonfire, and were generally not yet looking for boys.

Connie had applied for a scholarship for her junior and senior years at Loretto Academy in Niagara Falls. Alas, the application had been sent before she met Frank. She prayed to God all summer that she would not win this prestigous award, for fear of losing her first boyfriend. It was not to be, however, and at the end of July came notification that she had won a full scholarship, including books, room and board, all tuition, and any other expenses except her spending money. She was broken-hearted. I found this hard to understand, as this was something she had desired for some time. Not having experienced the joy of a first love, how could I know how she felt?

Our parents decided that even though everything was covered by the scholarship, the spending money would pose somewhat of a problem, and they were simply unable to find it in their limited budget. My sister Rita, who was a secretary at Canadian National Railways, volunteered to send Connie $2 a week (a substantial amount in those times) if that would help matters. That was just about enough, and our parents decided that Connie would accept the scholarship. Needless to say, Rita was in Connie's bad books for some time after that, for being instrumental in her having to leave her newfound beau. In September, Connie bade Frank McGrath and the rest of us a tearful goodbye and boarded the CNR train for Niagara Falls.

Connie was a model student, and fitted in well with the other girls who were from various parts of the world. She formed lasting friendships, still corresponds with four or five of her schoolmates, and returned to the school for the fiftieth anniversary of her graduation.

She was the valedictorian, won the Governor General's medal and met her future husband at that graduation. And Frank McGrath? Before Connie graduated, she received the news that Frank had been killed overseas, and we all shared her grief at the loss of a fine young man.

Our sister Rita, to whom Connie had made amends, decided she would use her CNR pass to visit Connie in Niagara Falls. She arrived on a Friday evening, and the Sisters placed her in a nicely decorated guest room to be shared with Connie. The head mistress greeted her warmly, and asked what their plans were for the next day. They recited the sights they planned to see. As the Falls were visible from the school, they didn't have far to go for their first item of sightseeing. They listed off the items chosen for the day, finishing off with a flourish – dinner in a fine restaurant. Sister Genevieve recommended the Rainbow Room at the General Brock Hotel, and they agreed to try it out. Unbeknownst to Connie, Rita was not in a position to pay for the fare at the General Brock, and during the day made several references to the fact that she would dearly love a hamburger. Finally Connie got the message and they shared a light meal at a small eatery. But what to tell Sister Genevieve? They decided they had better have a quick peek at the Rainbow Room. Arriving before the Saturday night patrons, they told the maitre d' that their mother was planning a wedding for Rita (who was engaged at the time) and they would like to see the Rainbow Room and look at the menu. He agreed, saying that this would usually be done by the banquet manager, who did not work on Saturday. As the Rainbow Room overlooked the Falls, the girls took their time, while taking in the view from all angles They agreed that when the maitre d' showed them the menu Connie would memorize the left side and Rita would do the same on the right.

Arriving back at the Academy, Sister Genevieve was enthralled with their stories of sightseeing, and finally the subject of dinner came up. They dwelt on the table they had chosen overlooking the Falls, and the delicious meal they had eaten. For Sister's benefit, Connie dwelt on the oysters on the half shell, rainbow trout, parsleyed potatoes, and garden vegetables that were cooked to perfection, their colours like a rainbow itself. Rita took over here and described the cherries jubilee, flaming like diamonds in the sunlight. They had a pot of tea that was served in a silver teapot, and was replenished many times as they sat and admired the spectacular view.

They were very convincing, and as they tell the story today, they don't even wonder why Sister was so entertained. They realize now that Sister didn't believe a word of it, but she didn't bat an eyelid at their marvellous performance.

Tearfully, Rita left the next day, having saved ten cents for the payphone in the CNR station in Montreal. This was desperately needed so that she could phone her fiance to tell him she had arrived, for he had offered to pick her up at the station.

Yes, I am sure Sister Genevieve may have written a story about this visit, and perhaps entitled it, "The Innocent Deception."

MORE MEMORIES

Our sister Phyllis entered the Convent of the Sacred Heart when I was eight or nine, so my memories or her are like wisps of fog that come and go. It was generally understood that Phyllis was Mum's right hand. She could do anything Mum could do, including sewing, embroidering and knitting. I can't even imagine how many socks she helped to darn. Phyllis always knew she was the appointed one to take over in an emergency if Mum was incapacitated in any way. I remember when Phyllis made a set of beautiful doll's clothes with which she dressed a lovely doll for Connie. I never told her I was terribly hurt that she had given a doll to Connie and not one to me, also. Years later, after I had a grandchild, Emily, I told Phyllis about this episode, which surprised and upset her. If you visit my house, you can find a beautifully dressed doll on a bed in a guestroom, a gift from Phyllis and hand-made to boot. I did allow my grandchild to play with it a few times, but that doll will always be a reminder of the goodness of Phyllis.

My sister Jean was ten years older than I, and my memories are few and far between. I grew to know her after she married and had children. At 3431 Rosedale, I remember watching from the stairway as Jean and Rita had parties — was it one party or many? It seems as though I was always on the fringe of something big. Phyllis tells stories of Jean in her early years, and Rita enlightens us about Jean's later years. I have enjoyed these stories, and they fit in exactly to my memory of the kind of person she was. When Jean entered a room, it lit up with her smile, her warmth and her beauty. I do remember that, and only later did I get to know the inner beauty of my sister Jean. She left us too soon when we had become fast friends. She left us a legacy in her seven children who remind me of Jean in so many ways — the eyes, the nod of a head, a laugh, a chuckle, a tear, and always great love and affection.

Christmas was a magical time for us as for most families. How did Santa manage so well to satisfy the needs of so many little ones? The magic was in the love and sacrifice of our mother (and I suspect Phyllis) who made sure that each one of us had something very special. I still picture the softly falling snow, the large fairy-tale snowflakes drifting by our magnificent living room windows. We watched from our cozy places, wondering when Santa would slide down our chimney. We knew he would not come until we were safely asleep. It must have been a relief to Mum when we asked to go to bed early. The real magic happened when we trundled down the stairs at five the next morning to the calls of, "He's been here!" Oh Happy Day!

New Year's Eve was a very special time. We would gather around the fireplace at 11.45 and say the Rosary. I remember this very well, because as we got older, if we were invited on a date, we had to make it clear that this ritual must be kept. I don't recall any refusals, as Mum always prepared a midnight feast that in Quebec is called *Reveillon*. I remember one time she cooked a piglet, and it was brazenly basking on a platter, sporting the traditional apple in its mouth. I think that was a one-time venture, but it was applauded and enjoyed by all.

To sum it all up, Rosedale Avenue had its joys and sorrows, but if there was a better home, we would be hard put to find it. Perhaps when in Montreal, you will drop by and revisit the scene of our childhood and reminisce with us, imagining snowbanks as high as an elephant's eye, and picture Dad's myriad roses that he was able to plant in later years, after our backyard had done its duty as baseball field and hockey rink. His philosophy was that playgrounds for children were more important than zinnias and honeysuckle or even roses. Nurturing of flowers could wait, if a choice had to be made. Our parents always made good choices.

COLONIAL AIRLINES

In 1941, there I was, working for Canadian General Electric, sorting the blue receipts from the red and putting things in numerical order. Having a mathematical bent, I soon figured out that anything with blue on it was good and anything with red was bad. I added up the blues and subtracted the reds on a daily basis (not part of my job) and soon figured out that my company was doing well. But was I? Finishing my assigned daily work in short order, I was always looking for something extra to keep me busy. I began keeping track of the stock, and became what I would now call a "gofer." Our office in Montreal was located on Beaver Hall Hill, and my newly married sister, Rita, and her husband lived in what I thought to be a "grand" apartment at 3410 Peel Street, just above Sherbrooke. The walk to the apartment was all uphill, and although it was quite an effort, I went there for lunch every day. Preparing lunch for me daily was an effort for her also, something I didn't realize in those days. She encouraged me, however, and we enjoyed being together.

En route to her home, I would pass the offices of Colonial Airlines, which featured a large model aircraft in the picture window. I was totally enthralled with this display, and made it a habit to drop in each week to ask about a job. After several weeks, the secretary called out to the president, who was ensconced in a mezzanine office, "I can't stand it any more, Mr. Shaughnessy, you will have to see this young lady." Mr. Shaughnessy stuck his head out over the mezzanine wall, and called down, "Come on up here." So started my pie-in-the-sky career in the travel business. Mr. Shaughnessy gave me a quick quiz of a general nature, and I passed. (I did not tell him how little I knew about his company or airplanes of any kind.) He told me it was unusual for him to hire an applicant, for he always handpicked (!) girls from other companies if they suited his fancy. He told me that his employees did not work for the money, but for the love of the job, and offered me $100 a month. I was so thrilled, I almost told him it was the most wonderful amount I had ever heard of, but I contained myself, and said that it would be suitable. After the gofer's $60 a month, visions of all kinds of purchases floated in my brain, but the thought of working for an airline obscured all others, and I felt I was the luckiest person in the world. I was sixteen. Mr. Shaughnessy had made it a point that he never, but never, hired anyone under twenty-one, and between the lines I heard, "So you had better measure up." I felt somewhat threatened, but vowed to do my very best to be an asset to Colonial Airlines.

There were two other young ladies, Frankie O'Brien (handpicked from Mappins) and Carol Graham (plucked from the Royal Bank), in addition to the secretary, Irene Hollosi, to whom I will always be grateful. I was trained in the tariffs, the pricing of flight legs, through-travel, connecting flights, comparison pricing, etc., and the only advice I was given was "Don't use the word 'Parachute'." I was a passenger agent who booked reservations, spoke to other offices via the teletype (we used a five-letter code which I presumed was for secrecy but of course was to decrease the cost of the message). We issued tickets, arranged special limousines, and checked in all passengers who used the regular limousines to the airport. We had to record the age, weight and baggage weight of every passenger. It was wartime, and we were also responsible for checking their documents, such as passports, visas, etc. After the limousine departed for the airport, we would call in the manifest to the airport agent. This was given to the captain of the airplane, who would manually add the weight of the people, baggage and fuel so the plane would not be overloaded. There were times when the total actual weight exceeded the allowable limit, and passengers would be deplaned for overload at the last moment before takeoff.

Many prominent people travelled with us, including celebrities, and I remember that Joan Crawford was very indignant when I asked her age. She taught me that c*elebrities* such as she had only to say the word "adult." (I'm no celebrity but I think that was good advice, and have used it since in certain situations.) I noted that her attitude was not the most gracious. In comparison, I remember that when Yehudi Menuhin missed the Colonial limousine and I had to order a "private limousine," he was most apologetic for putting *me* out. How different from one another we mortals are, and I was learning a lot from many mortals.

One day, an impresario whose name, I believe, was Norman Granz, entered our office, bursting with stunning show-biz news. A very special entertainer would be arriving from the airport, having flown in on our aircraft. That wasn't unusual, as we were the only US carrier and all American celebrities used our service if arriving from the States.

"You'll be thrilled when he steps out of the limousine at the side door of the Mount Royal because he'll wave at you if you stand at your side window. And guess what? I'm giving you two tickets to his performance tonight at the Verdun Auditorium." We were not overly impressed as our usual invitations were to the Normandy Roof. However, we thanked him graciously and humbly, advising him that we considered ourselves very lucky indeed to be able to attend this concert. We would be happy to use the tickets. After he left, we were hard pressed to find someone willing to go to the performance of an unknown singer. We didn't try to get a glimpse of him as he arrived at his hotel, for that would have meant keeping watch, which seemed like work. Frankie O'Brien and I were the lucky ones to get the tickets, and we agreed to have a bite to eat and proceed to the auditorium. Who was this Frank Sinatra anyway?

Came show time, and we were shocked to see this skinny little guy come out on the stage. As he adjusted the microphone to his height, he looked like a stagehand preparing for the arrival of the big star. And then he sang. His interpretation of the lyrics was unique, and he wooed his mainly female audience with a soft, silky, come-hither invitation that lifted most of the audience into another fantasy world. The satiny strains of "I'll Walk Alone" slid from Frank Sinatra's throat, and at that moment, a middle-aged woman, sitting directly in front of us, jumped up from her seat, climbed over about twelve enthralled onlookers, ran onto the stage, knelt down and grabbed the singer's leg, shouting, "You don't have to walk alone, Frankie, I'll walk wid ya, Frankie." And then it started. Screams came from all over the auditorium as did the fans. Pandemonium reigned supreme as the stage filled with crowds of bobbysoxers and what looked like their mothers. We were impressed with Frank Sinatra, but could not understand the riot he provoked. He continued to sing, as though nothing unusual was happening on the stage of the Verdun Auditorium. At the close of the concert, we remained in our seats, not wanting to be trampled by these out-of-control crazies.

Mr. Granz came into our office before he accompanied "Frankie" to the airport the next day, surprised that we were calm and collected after witnessing the show of a lifetime. We told him how impressed we were, and he offered to have Frankie wave to us from the hotel door as he entered the special limousine we had ordered. We feigned excitement at the prospect, and waved and smiled at the little fellow, who favoured us with a bow, a wave and a doff of his fedora. Were we blessed or what? Over the years, I learned to appreciate Frank Sinatra, the crooner and actor, but I never could shake the image of a poor, skinny, underfed singer.

During the war, the airline was obliged to remove passengers and give their seats to US ferry pilots who were travelling to US destinations where they would fly their assigned aircraft to Europe. This happened on a daily basis, and it was very frustrating for the ticketed passenger whose airline was the only one that flew trans-border from Montreal. I remember calling a passenger — the president of a company — and advising him that we needed his seat for a priority passenger. He called later, asked for me, and asked me if I would like to go for a coffee at the Honey Dew coffee shop next door to our office. I asked Mr. Shaughnessy, who replied "*Who* wants to buy you coffee?" I replied, "Mr. Noorduyn." Mr. Shaughnessy was very pleased and we concurred that Mr. Noorduyn understood our problem and was going to commiserate with me. He was president of Noorduyn Aviation, which was designing and building airplanes and was a VIP passenger for our airline and the war effort. My coffee with Mr. Noorduyn was somewhat disappointing, as I thought he was going to compliment me on my customer service approach. We spoke of many things, and finally he said, "I want to tell you something very important, something I want you to remember for the rest of your life." He looked me in the eye, and said, "You will catch more flies with honey than with vinegar." My approach had been less than perfect, and I understood immediately what he meant. I appreciated the time and trouble he took to give advice to a very young girl, and I never forgot his words or the man himself. He became my very important passenger, and although he lived in Vermont, he telephoned me to book all his hotel and airline reservations around the world for years to come. He died some years ago, and when I heard the news, telephoned his wife. She remembered the "airline girl." I told her then how her husband had helped me, and it seemed to give her some comfort.

About a week after I started my exciting new job, Mr. Shaughnessy, who usually asked his secretary to speak to the staff for him unless it was very urgent, approached me to say that I would be going to New York the following week — I was to be measured for my uniforms at Saks Fifth Avenue. This could not be happening to me! A dream comes true! I had always imagined that someday I would like to visit New York, Paris and Havana in that order. Thinking I had misunderstood Mr. Shaughnessy, I said, "You mean *go* to New York'?" He said gruffly, "That's what I mean, and I'll confirm your flights tomorrow." My legs started to wobble and, afraid I would faint, I quickly thanked him and sat down. I would be going on an airplane! I would be flying! The rest of the day I could think of nothing but the thrill that awaited me next week. I would wait until dinnertime to casually tell my family that I would be *flying* to New York on business the following week. They would all be happy for me, and how the news would spread among our friends and relatives. In 1941, flying was for the rich and idle, along with big-business men and Air Force pilots. It was certainly not for the likes of me, a sixteen-year-old who had dreamed of visiting New York in her old age — after her thirtieth year.

And so it arrived, the magic moment when I would announce that I had very good news to share. After dessert (apple pie, the family favourite), I took a big breath and calmly told of my good fortune. My siblings were thrilled for me, but I will never forget the looks on the faces of my parents. Their eyes never blinked, and their mouths remained open in horror. I think my father was shaking and for a few moments did not speak. When he did, it was with a calm determination. His words shattered all my dreams and my excitement, and I was too upset for tears, when he said, "You are too young to go to New York alone, and I have little respect for any boss who would expect this of a young lady your age. You will not be going to New York and that is final." Dad's decisions were always final, and not one of us would even venture to object.

As usual, I accepted my fate, but my next challenge was to inform Mr. Shaughnessy of my father's decision. How embarrassing! The next morning I told Dad that it was very upsetting for me to have to tell Mr. Shaughnessy that my father was making my decisions, especially when I had such an important job. Dad's reply: "You figure out the best way to do it, but you must do it immediately. Remember that part of your 'important job' is using the brain God gave you. Use it now to see that as a sixteen-year-old you will be in some danger alone in New York City. If you can't visualize this, then you must take my word for it, for I would never give you advice that is not in your best interest. We'll talk tonight."

How did he know how awful it would be to look into Mr. Shaughnessy's eyes and tell him my father would not permit me to go? What did he know about my co-workers (who had been to New York but were somewhat older than I) thinking of me as a baby? Well, I just couldn't do it, that's all. "Honesty is the best policy" is just a bunch of words. How could I explain it so that Mr. S. would not think I was still a child, living under the parental guidelines of old-fashioned people? If I was unable to go, then how would I get my uniforms, and would I be fired? With whom should I discuss this in order to get some ideas? All of these thoughts rattled around in my head, until Dad's words came back to me. I must speak to Mr. S. as soon as he came into the office. I must be prepared to go back to sorting the blue from the red and putting things in numerical order. Filing they called it — I called it "hell." Could I go to New York without my parents' knowing? Just thinking the thought was frightful — I could not attempt that deceit. And so it was Damn the Torpedoes, Full Steam Ahead — to what? To the end of a career ordained in Heaven — after only two weeks.

Oh God, look down on my agony, and give me an answer that will save my job and my dignity — but especially my job!

I have always thought that if you have to do something that is distasteful, and if you have given it enough thought, it is better to get it over with. It is usually "better," not "easier," for nothing makes it easy.

Mr. Shaughnessy, all 6 foot 3 of him, arrived at his usual time, and headed for his hideaway in the mezzanine. I gave him enough time to collect himself, then called up the back stairs, "Mr. Shaughnessy?" He answered gruffly as usual, "Yes." Oh, Lord, what had I done? "May I see you in your office for a moment, please?" Annoyed, "Yes." I trembled as I mounted the narrow stairs, and presented myself before the president. "What is it?" again annoyed. Oh, Lord, let this moment pass, and I will always make my bed. "Mr. Shaughnessy, it's about my trip to New York. I told my father about it. He is very old fashioned (what a barefaced lie) and does not want me to go to New York alone, as much as I wish to go." A big grin, "He doesn't, eh? Well, they don't call him 'Battling Vince' for nothing. Did I say you were going alone? Do you think I would allow you to go to New York all by yourself? No, Denise Laporte, our chief stewardess, will accompany you on the plane, and you will travel with Mr. Fred Perry, the Canadian diplomatic courrier. You will have to stay overnight at the Roosevelt Hotel, in a single room, but Mr. Perry will be next door and you will be very safe. Our people in New York will take over in the daytime, and Mr. Perry and Miss Laporte will accompany you on the return flight."

I was breathless. Ecstatic. Visions of telling General Electric that I would be unable to accept a job offer as gofer were flying around the air, and then there was no air, and I was falling straight ahead, fainting at the news. But what would Mr. Shaughnessy think if I fainted on his beautiful beige rug? I felt dizzy and could not utter a word. "Thank you, Mr. Shaughnessy," finally came out in a whisper, and I turned and went down the steps, clinging to the banister.

Several hours later I replayed the scene with great enjoyment, savouring every detail, but wait! How did Mr. Shaughnessy know that Dad was called Battling Vince? I would have to figure this out when my day at the office was finished, and I relaxed on the Number 3 streetcar that would deliver me to my corner.

BATTLING VINCE

Our father was born in a suburb of Ottawa in 1884, the son of Ellen Corrigan and school principal Patrick Braceland, and grew up on Cumberland Avenue in Ottawa. That address comes to mind because my sister Connie, who lives in South Carolina, was travelling onboard a flight to Montreal. She noticed that a hockey team was aboard, and sitting close to her was King Clancy, whom she recognized. She said to him, "I'm Vince Braceland's daughter." He stood up, kissed and hugged her, and said, "It was an honour to carry his skates. You take me right back to 610 Cumberland Avenue and Vince Braceland. He was the greatest defenceman I've ever seen. I watched him many times when he was captain of the "Emmetts" in Ottawa. I've heard about his work with athletes in Montreal, and because of his character it doesn't surprise me."

Dad worked in the public relations department of the Canadian National Railways, but is better known for his self-appointed volunteer work. He coached at nearby Loyola College, and was determined that neighbourhood boys have the same athletic opportunities that had been afforded him when he was young. When I was around five, he put his dream into action. Since there were no sports facilities in our neighbourhood, Dad made a baseball diamond in our back yard in the summer and an ice rink in the winter, watered the rink in all kinds of weather, refereed all games, and froze his hands and face many times. He set up the teams, coached, and held meetings in our dining room. The neighbourhood children played their beloved sports and Dad became a well-known and well-respected member of the community. Because equipment was not available to all prospective players, he "begged, borrowed and stole" (according to Mum) skates, pads, bats, mitts from any source he could. In the summertime our neighbours delivered their garden blooms to Mum, thanking her for her generosity in donating our yard to the kids in both summer and winter.

We had an interim park. Dad oversaw it, and several older athletes helped organize the teams, which would number seventy-five. I remember George Strickland, who later played for the Victorias, as being a big strong boy of seventeen and a dedicated supporter. But Dad had his eye on the large parcel of land across Sherbrooke Street. His question to the city fathers was — would they establish a park there that would include sports fields and facilities?

It took quite a few years of begging, cajoling, stubbornness, and doggedness, but finally in the early 1930s, the city give in to Battling Vince and established Trenholme Park. There were fields for baseball and football, an outdoor ice rink, clubhouse and changing rooms. He begged industry for donations to help supply needed equipment for the boys. This was much appreciated by their parents, some of whom had been hit hard by the Depression. Molson's was especially generous, supplying sweaters, socks and hockey pants, while Elmhurst Dairy supplied blankets for the boys on the bench. I had always thought that they were horse blankets, for after all, our milk was delivered by milkmen whose wagons were pulled by horses. My brother Hugh thinks the blankets were Hudson's Bay, but I prefer to stick with my horse blanket theory. There were other donations of skates, pads and hockey sticks. Where his athletes were concerned, Battling Vince did not take No for an answer.

My brother Hugh remembers some of the young men who played on one of the many teams in Trenholme Park: George Strickland for the Victorias, Kenny Mosdale for the Canadiens and Dickie Moore.

Dad was a friend of Basil, "Baz," O'Meara, the sports writer for *The Star*. They held many long discussions on the pros and cons of the Montreal Canadiens, for example, who should win the Conn Smythe trophy, the Lady Bing trophy or the Norris Trophy. I recently came across a letter from Baz, saying, "I knew Vince well, even in his hockey days. He was a great defenceman."

During the conversations with Baz, Dad would mention the names of his players and their opponents. He would name the outstanding players he considered outstanding and who should be moved up to the farm team or go right to the Canadiens or the Maroons. Teams looking for new youngsters invariably scouted Dad's talented players and their opposing team counterparts, among whom were Doug Harvey and Fleming Mackell. Dad thought Doug was the best defenceman he had ever seen, and he could pick 'em. The National Hockey League over the years has agreed with his opinion. He called Fleming Mackell a "Bullet," for never had Dad seen such speed on skates. Fleming, a centreman, had great stamina, and was a reliable penalty-killer. For a small hockey player, he was very powerful, and a tremendous asset to the Bruins and Maple Leafs.

I have long thought that there should have been a plaque in the memory of our father at Trenholme Park to commemorate the work he did for the community, with no thought of reward. Plaque or no plaque, his efforts will always be remembered by his family and those who benefitted by his generosity.

He was a true hero to many people. I well remember one morning the doorbell ringing at three a.m. A fifteen-year-old boy fell into our father's arms weeping and saying he had shot his stepfather. Dad was a safe haven in any storm. He was trusted because he would listen, and never broke a confidence. He was wise and kind, genuinely interested in the problems of others, and tried to be of help. In the case of this young man, I know he did whatever he could to ease the boy's pain, as well as the suffering of the family.

A new family moved into our neighborhood – a widow with four children. The widow heard about our father's success in working with young people in the area of sports. She met with him and told him the story of her three boys, who were being beaten up each day on the way to school, simply because they were unknown quantities in the eyes of the regulars who trod that path. Dad arranged for boxing lessons for all three, instructing them to tell no one, and to use different routes to school as often as possible until he gave them the word to use their skills. The eventful day arrived. All three were prepared as they took the route frequented by the regulars. When accosted, all three used their newfound art of boxing. No more fights occurred after that day, and our three boxers won the respect of their peers. That was the first of many victories for them. The oldest went on to become a dentist and practiced in the area for many years. The next two earned degrees as aeronautical engineers several years after my brother Hugh received his at Parkes Air College, a division of the University of St. Louis.

The boys' younger sister, Judy-Ann, was bedridden with polio. Dad dropped in to see her every day, stopping at the handy store to get her an ice-cream cone. She was to remember that kindness for the rest of her life. She told me that Dad's visit was the highlight of her day, as he told her stories about heroes. She recovered from polio, married and had her own family.

Some of my sisters' boyfriends also thought of our father as Battling Vince, when they sat on our side porch in the hammock and a booming voice would call out from the bathroom window above, "It's time you went home, young man." One admiring suitor remembered that after the first warning, Dad set the alarm clock in the bathroom, which was above the side verandah, and if the suitor hadn't left by the time the alarm stopped, Dad would throw out the clock to land nearby. It was a pretty solid clock, for it lasted for many such episodes. Maybe Mr. Shaughnessy had been one of these poor unfortunates who heard the lovely sound of Dad's alarm clock on one or more occasions. I would try to find out what the connection was.

I had four older sisters, and I approached Jean who was my senior by ten years. I asked her about how Mr. Shaughnessy might know of Dad's nickname. She asked me what Mr. S.'s first name was and I replied "Jack." Immediately she knew him. He was one of eight sons of Frank (Shag) Shaughnessy and was her age, twenty-six. She remembered him well, because when she was in grade school, Jack sat behind her and loved to dip her long blond curls in his inkwell. His father was a great friend of our father, and so of course Jack would know of the nickname. Strangely enough, Dad did not connect my boss with the Shaughnessy family he knew so well. No wonder! How could he have known all the names of Frank's eight sons, not to mention one daughter?

NEW YORK

The big day of my adventure in New York approached after several sleepless nights of anticipation. I boarded the limousine after work, and headed to Dorval Airport for Flight 5 to New York. On board, the head stewardess greeted me and showed me to my seat, where I was joined by a middle-aged man, who introduced himself as Fred Perry. After takeoff I proceeded to be astounded as the stars flew by. Mr. Perry gently corrected me, and informed me that what I was seeing was the plane's exhaust system working. The plane was a Douglas DC3, a twenty-one-passenger aircraft, and our flying time was 2 hours, 35 minutes non-stop for 313 air miles. That was long enough to become acquainted with Denise and Mr. Perry. On arrival in New York, Mr. Perry and I bypassed customs and immigration and proceeded to a private limousine, which was parked near the airplane. Mr. Perry ushered me to the limo and the driver opened the rear doors for us. As we seated ourselves, Mr. Perry introduced me to his permanent driver in New York by saying, "Show her your gat, Charlie." Mr. Perry had a large briefcase shackled to his arm, and because it was wartime, he carried secret documents between Ottawa and Washington, changing planes in Montreal and New York. He disengaged himself from the briefcase only when we reached the hotel and placed it in a safe, with Charlie guarding him at all times. How exciting! This was an extra adventure I had not imagined, and it was getting better all the time.

Mr. Perry asked me if I liked Guy Lombardo. Of course I did. Many a New Year's Eve we listened as he played in the new year — all from *New York City!* I enthused over his music, and Mr. Perry asked me if I would like to hear him, for his was the orchestra at dinner in the Roosevelt Hotel. I could not refuse, but on the other hand it meant I would be with Mr. Perry, and I doubted if my parents would approve. After I checked into the hotel, I immediately phoned long distance to ask permission of my parents. They said yes, as they had had a talk with Mr. Shaughnessy.

We had a delicious dinner in the hotel, wonderfully served, and listened to the sweet strains of Guy Lombardo — a dream come true. Mr. Perry acted like a father, and I was grateful that Mr. Shaughnessy had chosen so well. Mr. Perry had his job until the war ended, and called me at least once a week on his way through Dorval Airport just to say hello. He was my introduction to New York, which I was to visit many times during my years with the airlines, but no visit measured up to my first experience.

The next day my name should have been Cinderella. I was escorted from the hotel to the Colonial Airlines office at 51 Vanderbilt Avenue to meet the President and staff, with whom I would be working via the Teletype. Off then to Saks Fifth Avenue for the fitting. I was shown the finished product - - a forest green suit with four blouses, an all-weather coat and a forage cap in grey tinged in forest green and red. The forage cap sported Colonial's gold wings. I fell in love with this uniform, for its lines were clean and sharp. Mine was obviously going to fit perfectly when the tailors at Saks had done their job.

On the flight home, I felt like a veteran traveller - - there is not much for a passenger to learn on a DC3. Still I was awed with the thought that we were travelling high above the clouds and carrying on very mundane conversations when the heavens surrounded us and we were so far from reality. How I admired the pilot for delivering us with such perfect precision to the runway reserved for Flight 8 from New York. We had been taught that we were statistically seven times safer in the air than on the ground, and I never once doubted it, then or now. I was at home on Colonial Airlines Flight 8. It was the end of a perfect day. *Adieu* to Denise and Mr. Perry who had been such wonderful companions, and I hoped we would meet again.

The next two years were growth periods for the airline and for me. New staff was hired, but where to put them? Exit Mr. Shaughnessy, gone from his mezzanine hideout to a private office on Peel Street. How we would miss our handsome hero, our protector, our Boss.

Frankie O'Brien, Carol Graham, Patty O'Brien, and I stayed on the ticket counter and new reservation agents were installed on the mezzanine. Previously our *modus operandi* had been to ask the client pertinent information: name, contact and flights, which we would write on a 3x5 card. We would then enter his name in pencil on the appropriate chart. If he cancelled later, we would simply rub out his name on the chart and draw an X on his 3x5 card. With the new reservation agents now on deck, we would have to ask them regarding the availability of the flights we wanted. Someone came up with a novel idea, and we used it for a year: filling out the 3x5 card, we would call up to the mezzanine, saying, "Reservations." An agent would drop a cord over the balcony. Attaching our card to the cord with a paper clip, we would send up the request, which would return a few minutes later with the flights marked as "OK," or if the flights were not available, the agent would call out, "Waiting List, any alternate?" And so it would go until all space was confirmed. The passenger at the desk would look like a kid bobbing for apples, as his head went up and down following the action.

When I was nineteen, I was appointed to the acting manager of reservations. The "acting" was so that I could be replaced when the men came back from the war, for as a general rule, women did not hold management position sixty years ago. I didn't even think that far into the future, for I was perfectly happy training new personnel in my favourite subject, "customer service," and calming irate passengers when they were either deplaned for priority or delayed or cancelled due to weather or mechanical problems. In those days, however, people tended to be more patient and polite than they are now. Flying was still a fairly new adventure, and was viewed as a status symbol. If you were going to *fly* somewhere, you must be an important person. This attitude did not really change until the 747s were introduced and flying became as routine as bus or train travel.

VISITORS & PASSENGERS

During my time at Colonial Airlines (which was destined to become Eastern Airlines) we always kept a courtesy phone on the counter for the convenience of our passengers. When I started there, I noticed that a very disheveled gentleman would look around before he entered, then shuffle over to the telephone, dial, say a few words, and then with a furtive glance around, scurry out the door. I asked my co-workers if they knew who he was. They replied that he was almost a mascot for us. He was Jockey Fleming, whose office was a little chalk mark on the sidewalk at the corner of Peel and Ste. Catherine Streets. They whispered to me that should a passenger want a bottle of scotch or other liquor after hours, Jockey Fleming was the man. I was to learn volumes about the world and its inhabitants just by observing the happenings on that corner. The spot still engages my attention and when I drive by, I feel I have come home again. Jockey Fleming very obligingly placed bets for our "in-the-know" passengers, for I believe that was his main occupation. Many in the area knew him by name, passed the time of day with him, and passed on a few dollars after briefly and quietly discussing the details.

I was not familiar with nightlife, but Jockey Fleming came to my rescue on many occasions when I worked the evening shift. Passengers arriving from New York would come into the office asking about a good place to eat or have a drink and go dancing. He always recommended the most reliable places for our passengers, knowing that we would be there the next day to tell him a story that was pleasant or unpleasant, depending on his recommendation. I believe he was also protecting his telephone privileges! Several years ago, *The Gazette* devoted a whole page to Jockey Fleming, on the occasion of his death. For me he will live on forever, as I recall his comings and goings, and my introduction to a way of life that was foreign to me. I do know that Jockey Fleming added a dimension to my thinking, allowing me to enlarge my circle of thought, to see things from a different perspective, and to be curious about how others live.

Another frequent visitor to our office was a man by the name of Mr. Bernard D. When I worked from seven a.m. to three p.m. on Sunday, I was never shocked to see Mr. D., strolling down Peel Street with a goose on a leash. He would spend Saturday night in the Mount Royal Hotel, and when his liquor was finished, would totter down the street and enter our office. In a loud voice, he would say, "I'm drunk. Call my uncle, the chief of police, and tell him to get a car down here pronto to take me home." The first time it happened I was reluctant to call the station, though we had their number handy in case of a break-in. However, I had not been told that this occurred every Sunday morning, and I was a little nervous being alone with him in his condition. I reasoned, however, that he really loved the goose, and would not do anything rash while he had the bird with him. I finally called the station, gave the police his message, and they assured me that the chief would take care of it. Sure enough, a few minutes passed, and along came a police car, which parked on Mount Royal Place, a more discreet location then Peel Street. Mr. D doffed his hat, thanked me in a most gentlemanly fashion, straightened his back, and proceeded out the door, giving his friend a yank on the leash to alert him that they were on the move. A Sunday without Mr. D would have been considered a dull day indeed, but it never happened.

One day I called a passenger in the Mount Royal Hotel (we had a direct line to the operator) to advise him that he had been deplaned for a priority passenger. I heard an awful noise and what sounded like gurgling. I held onto the line, and using an outside line, called the operator, informing her that I believed the person in room 7008 had had a heart attack. She sent someone to the room immediately. The passenger was screaming at the telephone that he had just pulled out of the wall. He was in good health, but was suffering from something akin to road rage –- deplanement rage! It was his third deplanement in as many days, and he *just wasn't going to take it any more!* The diagnosis was switched to hotel rage, when he was informed that the telephone and room damages would be added to his bill.

Many of our clients believed that if they offered us nylon stockings we would change their deplanement and hand if off to someone else. Anyone who did this was automatically moved to the bottom of the waiting list as far as we were concerned. We didn't like the idea of being bribed, but at Christmas we weren't averse to accepting a few gifts from loyal passengers. Most of the presents were in the form of very choice alcohol and we had to make a few trips home because of their huge number and their weight. Perhaps they thought we were all alcoholics. No, I think they just appreciated our good service, and were thinking about future deplanements, and how to protect themselves.

When deplaned, one passenger said that his partner had not been called, and he would produce nylons if we would remove his partner and let him go. He did not know that the army had requisitioned the whole plane. We called the partner who was at the Mount Royal and told him that we were deplaning him. Guess what – he offered up his partner. We wondered how long these two would stay together.

GAMBLING

One of our senior pilots was Sam Barnett. Sam lived in New York, but loved Montreal. He would bring Flight 6 to Montreal, and would turn it around and fly back to New York as Flight 5. We always knew if there was the slightest hint of bad weather anywhere on the system, Sam would cancel the flight. We assured the passengers that it was because we took the greatest safety precautions. Although he had up until one hour before departure to cancel, long before that we knew his flight would not operate if there was one weather disturbance — anywhere in the world! The flight superintendent at LaGuardia Airport would issue a statement saying that the flight *might* not operate, but we knew better. When the flight had been cancelled, Sam and the crew would arrive at our office, go in the back room and play a game of craps with dice. We always had rooms at the Mount Royal for stranded crews, and they would move the party over there after our office closed.

One day they asked me if I would like to roll the dice. I declined, not wanting to get involved in gambling of any sort. They convinced me that I should do it just for the fun. I ended up winning $8 and promptly went to the Jaeger store across the street and bought a sweater I had admired in their window. I showed the new purchase to my parents, and told them about the game. They made me take back the sweater and pay back those from whom I had won the money. I returned the sweater and put an envelope containing $8 in my ticket drawer. The next time Captain Barnett came in I gave him the money and asked that he return it to the other crew members. He could not believe his ears, saying, "This would *never* happen in New York." Later on that month, I visited Jaeger again and bought that purple sweater, but I never had the decadent feeling I had had when buying it with ill-gotten gains! I never again gambled with the crew in the back office of Colonial Airlines or anywhere else.

My next gambling venture was in Tampa, Florida, thirty-five years later, when I was with a group of travel agents at the dog races. One of the travel agents told me to bet on Rusty in the second. I approached the wicket and asked for "Rusty," placing $2 on the counter. The man said in a loud voice, "Rusty's the rabbit, lady." How mortified I was. I looked around to see if the trickster, Larry Libman, was in earshot, but I didn't see him. I asked the wicket man who was the favoured dog. He was most annoyed to be held up this way, suggesting I might want to have a look at the Odds board, if I thought I might be able to find it. He did say "Blackbird" looked good, but from the sneering look on his face, I doubted he believed it. Perhaps it was payback time for my holding him up. I did bet a few dollars on Blackbird, though, and collected a tidy sum. That evening at dinner, our host, Delta Airlines' Hank Canvin, had not as yet ordered the wine for our table. Tracking down the *sommelier,* I ordered wine, instructing him that if anyone inquired as to who had sent it, or even if they didn't, he was to say, "Compliments of Rusty." Larry Libman told everyone about the joke he had played on me, we all had a good laugh, and I think of "Rusty the Rabbit" every time I happen to run into Larry.

THE GENERAL

When I had been at Colonial Airlines for a few weeks, I answered the telephone and a man with a deep voice asked to speak to Mr. Shaughnessy. It was Mr. S.'s policy to have us screen all his calls. I asked who was calling, and he said, "General Eisenhower." My reply was, "Certainly, General, I'll transfer your call," which I did. I was trembling with excitement. I knew that Mr. Shaughnessy was a very important person, and this belief had just been strengthened. Was he a spy? All the billboards said, "Loose lips sink ships." Well, I certainly didn't want any ships sunk on my account. Imagine the secret I was keeping! I would endanger no one, and go to my death if necessary to guard what I knew to be life or death information. As the weeks went on, the calls became more frequent, and I recognized the voice every time. I never said the name out loud for fear of betraying the secret. If Mr. Shaughnessy had another call, I would creep up the back stairs to the mezzanine, and hold up my hand to signal that he should put his call on hold for a moment. With great solemnity I would whisper, "The General on line 2, Mr. Shaughnessy." Mr. S. would sign off immediately and take the call. I would scurry down the stairs, tempted to hold my ears in case I should hear a war secret and have a heavier burden to bear. How long could I keep this up?

Finally, I whispered the secret to Dad, who said it was incredulous. He thought about it for a moment, and asked me if I knew who General Eisenhower was. I replied that I had seen newsreels, which told of him being in charge of the European war theatre and that he

49

and Churchill were going to rid Europe of Hitler and his gang of thugs. "All well and good, but do you think General Eisenhower would be calling your Mr. Shaughnessy?" I thought about that and ventured a guess that Mr. S. was a spy for the Americans, and was keeping the general informed in some way or another. Not wanting to burst my bubble, Dad suggested that I keep on doing what I was doing, but to watch the progress of Eisenhower by reading all the newspapers I could get my hands on. I was never convinced that General Eisenhower was not closely associated with Jack Shaughnessy, especially when Mr. S. ran the Canadian part of the airline that carried so many US airmen and soldiers. Suddenly the phone calls stopped; this was around D-day. I felt that the general had no more use for the services of Jack Shaughnessy, and I missed his calls.

Some months later, a little old wizened man in his sixties entered our office and asked for me. I asked what I could do for him. He said, "I am General Eisenhower!" He grinned a sheepish grin and my war effort was shattered. He confessed that he was president of the advertising firm with whom we worked, and a friend of Jack Shaughnessy. He said it had all been a joke at the expense of Colonial's youngest employee, me, and it had offered many amusing moments. He apologized for himself and Mr. S, knowing that Mr. Shaughnessy's nature would not permit an apology. Ed Goodeve was his name. I dismissed the whole episode as just another experience into the ways of people, although I was somewhat shocked to find that grown men in important corporate positions could be so silly. I knew then the meaning of the expression, "Boys will be boys."

BILL

As the war was coming to a close, our business increased rapidly. More and more individuals felt the urge to try the latest mode of transportation. Businesses realized that they could profit from timesaving — it eliminated hotel and road expenses for their sales people. Consequently, Mr. Shaughnessy hired some new employees. Frankie O'Brien's sister, Patty, was hired. Frankie was a tall green-eyed brunette with features not unlike the actress Vivian Leigh. Frankie, however, was not just a beauty. She was an extremely intelligent person who had the ability to charm the most irate of passengers. Her sister, while possessing similar personality traits, was a stunning, statuesque blonde. Her infectious smile, along with her blue-green eyes could melt the hardest of hearts. They would become legends in the airline industry.

Then along came Bill. He seemed to be quite capable and friendly with everyone in the company. Passengers enjoyed his friendly manner. Bill wasn't always on time, but could smoothly find his way out of any criticism that was likely to come his way. One New Year's Eve I was working the day shift, and Bill was supposed to arrive at two o'clock to relieve me. At three, I realized that Bill was not going to show up at all. This meant I would have to fill in for him until ten at night. I was not happy to be working on New Year's Eve, but decided to make the best of it. About five o'clock, the florist arrived with a dozen long-stemmed red roses, with a card reading, "To the girl on the day shift, from the boy on the night shift, Love Bill." Only Bill could think that his charming ways could erase any ill feeling someone could have for him and his misdeeds. Bill finally left the airline, to go on to great things in Toronto, and we lost track of him.

The boy on the night shift was to turn up several years later, however, when I was working for Northeast Airlines (now Delta) in the Mount Royal Hotel. On a beautiful sunny June morning, a nattily dressed Bill appeared, wearing a beige shantung summer suit, a brown, beige and yellow paisley tie, highly polished shoes, and his famous heart-warming smile. We exchanged pleasantries for a few minutes, the conversation being mostly about how Bill had missed the airline and particularly the "Old Gang." How could I have forgotten the "Old Gang" — was there something I had missed? After softening me up with these reminiscences, he explained that he was registered at the hotel, and was making a big sales presentation in his suite to several important prospective clients. He was slightly short of cash and wondered if I would lend him the small sum of $50 for a few days until he could send it to me from Toronto. He actually convinced me that $50 was a very small amount, even though $50 at hand was a luxury I had never possessed, having to live from payday to payday, succumbing happily to the slick marketing skills of the Peel Street merchants.

Bill suggested that I cash a cheque for him, and this seemed to be the solution, for how could I let an old co-worker down, someone from the "Old Gang," especially when he was so close to firming up such a big transaction. In those days the hotels did not cash out-of-town cheques for their guests on the spot, and charged a large fee for their investigative efforts. Bill signed a cheque with a flourish, and I accepted it, handing over the $50. Several days later our accounting office in Boston advised me that the cheque had not been honoured by the bank. Since this was my first experience of this kind I did not think of it as "bouncing," a term which became quite familiar to me over my years in the industry. My instructions were that I was to replace the $50 with a special deposit at the bank by the end of the business day.

I tried to reach Bill at his office, but they had never heard of him. I tried to trace him by calling information, but nobody with his name was listed in Toronto. What was I to do? Dad was on a business trip — a CN cruise to Alaska — and Mum was with him. I could never ask a friend for money, having been brought up with the Shakespeare adage, "Neither a borrower nor a lender be." How about the Household Finance Company? They were always giving out the message that they were approachable, and at the moment I needed an approachable friendly person who had the resources I required. I could not approach my bank — it was also the company bank — for I knew too many people in the Peel Street branch of the Royal, and this was a very private matter. Approach the approachable I did, and within minutes had a crisp new $50 bill in my hand, which I attached to a deposit and my day was saved.

Within a few days, I called a family friend who was a lawyer. I told him the story and he agreed to follow up when he had received the details in writing, along with a copy of the cheque rejection, which I forwarded to him. He called me to say he would try to locate charming Billie, and would be in touch. Months passed, and I finally got a call from Guy Drummond, the lawyer. He asked if I would care to have a bite of supper with him, and then he would take me to Bill. I was ecstatic. Bill was going to pay me back, and I could pay off the $50 loan, which I was repaying at the hefty sum of $5 a month. Dragging the story out of Guy was like pulling teeth. He wanted my meeting with Bill to be a surprise, and it was.

We found Bill at a run-down motel on Upper Lachine road. It was called Cheerio Cabins, and Bill was slinging hash there and had been for months. The lawyer told me that the last known transaction of Bill's was to sell his mother's piano in order to replenish his liquor stock. Bill flashed his million-dollar smile, as he signed a promissory note for the amount owed. In my naiveté I fully expected that he would honor his promissory note, for after all it was his word. As the weeks and months passed with no payment from Bill, I realized that my anger had turned to compassion for a person who had never learned the meaning of the words "truth" and "work ethic." I accepted the fact that Bill's word would never mean anything to him or anyone else, as long as the bottle was his first love. As for Guy Drummond, he would not accept payment for his services, claiming he had been amused by the tenacity a young girl had shown over such a paltry sum. Everything's relative.

BUZZ

Going back to my days at Colonial Airlines on Peel Street, I recall that there were a few romances going on around me. Mr. Shaughnessy had hired several new people, one of whom was Katie Harris from Winnipeg. Her main concern was her tendency to gain weight just by going into the Honey Dew coffee shop next door. She really worked on keeping her figure trim, but with so many passengers inviting her for lunch, (a favourite place was "Desjardins") it was no easy task. Katie was my idea of the typical Irish colleen, with a wide-eyed expression and large green eyes. She had long, black, naturally curly hair, which had a will of its own, and used a little of that men's "greasy kid stuff" to keep it in tow.

Katie finally whittled down her array of boyfriends to just one. We couldn't understand the attraction, but she seemed to be enamoured of this tall, blond, serious character. He seemed eccentric to us, but he was devoted to Katie, and so we lent our approval. We had been introduced to George Beurling, but did not realize that he was "Buzz" Beurling, Canada's greatest war ace. He was called the "Falcon of Malta" and the "Knight of Malta." He won the Distinguished Service Order, the Distinguished Flying Cross, the Distinguished Flying Medal and Bar — all by the time he was twenty-one years of age. After Katie left the airline, I lost track of her, but by then the romance had been over for some time. I found out that Buzz had been killed in 1948 in a plane crash on his way to Israel to fly for and fight with the new State of Israel. Having read the book, *Hero: the Story of Buzz Beurling, Canada's Legendary Fighter Ace*, there is no mention of Katie in Buzz's life. The book says that Buzz was married in 1944, and was deeply in love with another American woman shortly after that — all at the same time that he was seeing Katie.

On Buzz Beurling's honeymoon, according to the story, they stayed with Freddie deMarigny in his Ste. Adele chalet. Marie Alfred Fouquereux de Marigny — "Freddie" to his friends — was known to the public as the man who stood accused, and later acquitted, of the murder of Sir Harry Oakes, the Canadian mining tycoon. Freddie was married to Harry's eighteen-year-old daughter, Nancy. When Harry was found murdered in his bed in Nassau, the Bahamas, Freddie was arrested for the deed. After he was acquitted, he arrived in Ste. Adele. The author asks the question "How did Buzz Beurling hook up with Freddie deMarigny?" It is a mystery that I am about to unravel. Famous Freddie was having a romance with our own Irene Hollosi, Mr. Shaughnessy's secretary — who had insisted that he see me, when I was sixteen and desperately wanted to work in that Peel Street office. Of course, George "Buzz" Beurling knew Marie Alfred Fouquereux de Marigny — they met in our office, proving the theory that if you stay long enough on the corner of Peel and Ste. Catherine Streets, you will meet everyone in the world.

NORTHEAST AIRLINES

In 1944 when I was nineteen, I became acting manager of reservations. Of course, 1944 was still a time of war, so the "acting" remained. Our Peel Street office was not large enough to house the fourteen people whom we would now need to fill all the reservation spots available, so very regretfully I gave up the direct contact I had with our passengers at the ticket counter on Peel. We set up a telephone reservation system in the lower lobby of the Mount Royal Hotel. Not by my design, my desk was on a podium where I could see every employee, and I was somewhat embarrassed by this. I no longer felt part of a team, but soon realized that now I was the coach of a new team, and my example would be an important part of my new job.

Several months after my appointment, Northeast Airlines was authorized to fly between New York and Montreal via Boston and vice versa. They sent their vice president of sales to Montreal to choose someone to set up their offices. Mr. George Scott decided that Canadian Air Express, the company for whom I worked, would handle all Montreal operations. He obtained the authority to observe our reservation office in action. At the end of a week, Mr. Shaughnessy, our boss, told me that Mr. Scott would like me to open the Northeast office, but it would mean cutting all ties with my first love, Colonial Airlines. It was a hard choice to make, but considering the extra benefits offered to me by Northeast, I could not refuse this offer, and so Northeast Airlines became the next love of my life. I hired two reservation agents, opened another office in the lower lobby of the Mount Royal Hotel, this one somewhat further from the Piccadilly Lounge, which at that time was located in the lower lobby. It would be tough sledding, trying to build the business of a new airline, especially in those times when flying was not the accepted method of transportation. I welcomed the challenge however, and so began my second job in the airline industry.

After several months, the inevitable happened. A district sales manager was appointed, and I would be reporting to this person — a man, of course, and a war veteran to boot. I was content with this arrangement, but it did not last long, for he and I were not compatible. He had no experience in the field, yet changed most of the rules, refused to allow me to travel on my pass, and in general, without any knowledge of the day-to-day business, made decisions that I felt came from his ignorance, not his acumen. This experience soured my view of my job and the airline industry, and I resigned, taking a job with Bell Canada as a trainee for a position as a service representative.

My life at the Bell would have been perfect, except for the fact that my heart longed for the excitement of the airline business. I felt that asking a customer what date he or she would be moving, and arranging for the installation of a telephone —either an 1RH or a 2RH, the latter being a party line, plentiful in those days of scarce equipment — was most boring, and I longed to return to the airlines. Airline jobs for girls were scarce then, for all positions were being offered to men returning from the war.

HOMES AWAY FROM HOME

I read in *The Star* that Northeast Airlines had purchased a new aircraft, and it was coming from Boston to Montreal on a promotional tour. It was a Convair, a ship new to me, and I immediately decided to visit Dorval Airport to see this phenomenon. At the airport, Mr. George Scott, the vice president of Northeast, deplaned from the Convair and noticed that I was in the front row of the crowd. He came over to visit with me, asking about my new career. I must have had a very sad face, for he said, "You don't like the telephone business much, do you?" It was all I could do to hold back the tears, as I replied that he was quite right. He asked me if I was interested in returning to the airline, and I said I certainly would but not under the same conditions. I gave him my home phone number, and he said he would see what was happening in Montreal and give me a call. That was my lucky day, and I always considered the Convair as my charmed aircraft.

True to his word as always, George Scott phoned me within the week, and said that he just couldn't find a spot in Montreal at the moment, for my ex-boss was still at the helm. He asked me to go to Moncton for the summer, and then to Boston until a position in Montreal became available. I detected that it would not be too long before I would be transferred home. I jumped at the opportunity, and gave thanks to the Bell Telephone Company for the excellent customer service training they had given me, and sorrowfully said good-bye to the nice people I had met there.

In Moncton, the airline paid all my expenses for the summer and put me up at the Queen's Hotel, which was close to the railroad station, and from which the airline limousine left for the airport. It was a homey place, and helped me cope with the loneliness of being away from home for the first time. The airline employees were friendly as only Maritimers can be, and invited me to all their parties and outings. The Moncton office was not a busy one, and I found that I was at loose ends most of the time, with not enough customers to assist, and no problems to solve. It was a pleasant time though, and I was able to see all the sights of that little town, including Magnetic Hill, the tidal bore and other wonders.

In September I was transferred to Boston, and managed to find a room in Winthrop, a stone's throw from Logan Airport. I also found a roommate, Muriel Luthie, a stewardess from New York, who used the room only for airline overnights, spending all her days off in New York. The room was postage-stamp size, and I was sometimes happy to be alone. Upstairs from us were two male university students who became good friends. None of us was allowed to step outside our room, except to leave or enter the house. Our landlady, a twenty-three-year-old business woman, had made it clear that her interest in us was only for the $10 a week that was to be paid on time, and so we spent as little time as possible at home.

Across the street lived a family with two children, and my great joy was to visit them. They often invited me for a meal, and I spent many hours enjoying the company of the little ones. I played the piano for them and particularly remember their many requests for "Zippity Doo Dah." I played by ear, having had no formal training on the piano, but they were a wonderful audience, and I knew mistakes would not be noticed. We danced together, sang together, and when they tired somewhat, I told many stories of princes and princesses, teddy bears and toads. Their story-books were well worn, and at the end of the day, nothing gave me more pleasure than to read to them, sometimes covering the same story two or three times. I was asked to baby-sit the children for a fee, but I refused, not wanting to change my status from friendly visitor to paid employee. The invitations to visit them continued throughout my stay in Boston, which helped to ease the pain of loneliness.

I became very friendly with the upstairs university students. We would eat dinner together at a family restaurant. I will always remember their Friday evening unvarying menu of Boston baked beans and brown bread. It was cheap and filling, and became our Friday ritual, before attending a movie.

Being from Canada, it was assumed that I was a good skater, for on my days off I came home to Montreal, carrying new white skates that I had never used. My skating had been on my brother's skates, and the blades did not have tines that the fancy skates possessed. My student friends asked me if I would go skating with them at Boston Gardens. I, of course, agreed and as they had never been on skates, asked me to go first and show them how it was done. I did so, taking a very long stride onto the ice, landing with a terrible bang, which knocked me out for a moment or two. It was impossible to get up without help and the evening ended with the boys all but carrying me home. It was a mortifying experience and a humbling one. Our landlady paid no attention to the fact that I was confined to bed. The boys called a local doctor the next day, and he very kindly came over to see me. I had bruised ribs that would have to heal on their own, and I was to stay in bed. The boys brought me dinner that night, and every night thereafter until I was up and around. To my surprise the doctor's wife brought my lunch every day. How kind she was, and I will always remember her and her husband. The boys had a field day telling the story of their Canadian ice-skating friend who couldn't handle Boston Gardens. I still went home on my days off, but I never carried those skates over my shoulder again. Another lesson learned: Pride goeth before a fall.

At long last came the transfer to Montreal. In one way, I was reluctant to leave Boston. The people I met had gone out of their way to befriend me, inviting me to their homes, and generally extending their hospitality above and beyond anything I could have expected.

HOME AGAIN

In my new job, I would be working in the Mount Royal Hotel managing the Northeast Airlines ticket counter and acting as assistant to the new sales manager, Hank Canvin. Managing the ticket counter was somewhat of an overstatement, inasmuch as I would be the only one working there. Back in my familiar surroundings, I was ecstatic, as was my family. I knew all of the sales people in the hotel, all the employees, and in general felt I had come home to the Mount Royal Hotel.

Early one morning, a passenger approached my counter, asking to check in on the next flight to Boston. As it happened, we had no record of him and there was no space. He became irate and shouted profanities at me. Grabbing me by my uniform collar, he lifted me off the floor and pulled me over the counter, pounding my chest on it until I was breathless and in a fair amount of pain. Fortunately, the Canadian Pacific counter wasn't far away, and the agent there came to my rescue. Gordie Lloyd was over six feet tall, and was a very strong man. He disengaged the claws of my passenger, lifted him off the floor, and dropped him on his feet with a bang. The passenger then turned his wrath on Gordie, as I called the hotel security. It turned out that the passenger had been attending a conference in the hotel and having partied all night, was very drunk. The security officer led him away, and Gordie and I closed our counters and had a coffee. I told Gordie that maybe I should go back to the 1RH and the 2RH at Bell Telephone. Nobody could hit me over the phone. He thought I should stay where I was because when passengers hit me, he could come to the rescue, thus releasing all his hostilities over his underpaid job.

That evening I discovered that my chest was blue, turning black, although the pain was not great. Only the next day did I feel as though I had been run over by a truck, but of course I had to be on duty at the ticket counter.

During my time at Northeast Airlines, we did a lot of advertising to familiarize the public with air transportation. Pictures were taken of me at our ticket counter, at the airport, and in other spots, always with a happy passenger in tow. The advertising agency used these in all their ads, and only now do I wonder why I was not paid for modelling services. My time and talents were volunteered by the airline, and no doubt the advertising agency saved quite a bit by accepting the offer, the agreement to which I was not privy. As I look at the glossy prints now, I think they should have paid the extra money for a model. I guess they wanted an honest to goodness "down-home" quality to represent our friendly airline. They goofed.

I posed with Montreal Mayor Camilien Houde in his office and can't remember the reasoning behind this shoot, but I believe it was used to promote Northeast Airlines as a good corporate citizen.

DISCRIMINATION

It was closing time at the Northeast Airlines Mount Royal Hotel ticket office in Montreal. I managed the ticket counter along with my other duties as assistant to the district sales manager. Having ascertained that all my passengers were out of the Piccadilly bar and safely installed in the airport limousine, I was about to leave the ticket counter and hop aboard the limo for my ride home, when a gentleman approached the counter, and I knew I would be streetcar bound again. He looked a bit down at heel, so perhaps he only wanted directions to the men's room, if I was lucky. However, I was prepared to give him the best service I could provide, as was the policy of my beloved airline.

And so I expected to issue a ticket or make reservations for this gentleman, even if it meant missing the drive with my passengers. The man was somewhat shy, but asked, "Do you have reserve stewardesses here in Montreal?" "Flight attendant" was a term not yet in use, as all cabin personnel were female. I replied that all our cabin personnel were stationed in Boston, and came to Montreal only on turnaround flights, but, "Is there a problem I can help solve?" I knew instinctively that I would not get a yes-or-no answer and so I waited for him to verbalize his position as I studied him more closely. He was of average height, black, handsome, somewhat morose, unsmiling, and with little worry lines like bird tracks spread across his forehead. He explained that his wife was pregnant with their second child, and the first, a little girl of seventeen months, would have to be transported to New York to be looked after by his sister while his wife was in the hospital, a matter of about a week.

Under his arm, he carried some worn-out magazines. I wondered what they contained and, as if to prove his credentials, he showed me the cover of a tired *Life Magazine* as he told me his name. He was Dr. Philip Edwards, and the cover photos clearly were of a happy carefree boy-man who was certainly a younger edition of the gentleman standing before me. He showed me his identification and, still shy and embarrassed, said he was sorry to have to ask for help. He was unable to get time off from his hospital job to do the trip himself, and even if he succeeded, the cost of losing pay and the airfare would be prohibitive for him. He would also worry about leaving his family alone at this critical time.

Is this what had happened to Dr. Phil Edwards, Canadian winner of a bronze medal for track in the 1932 Olympics, three bronzes in Los Angeles and one in Berlin? It was at the Berlin games that his team defied Hitler and gave the Olympic salute instead of the Nazi salute. Were a few minutes of fame and a spread in *Life Magazine* all that was left to remind us of Canada's most decorated Olympian? Where were family and friends, to help out in their time of need? What about his colleagues and neighbours? Tripping off my tongue like ripe apples falling from a tree, I found words like, "I would consider it a pleasure to take your little girl to New York," and "Oh, no, it will be no trouble at all," and "Absolutely not, I will do it on my days off "

Barely twenty, I thought I could handle this with one hand tied behind my back, such is the confidence of youth. I was the last of seven children, living at home, and would discuss this with my parents when I returned from work by streetcar. Dad was a wise man, who thought things out carefully before he put his stamp of approval on them. When I told him, he thought I had overstepped the boundaries of good sense, for after all, what did I know about these people? Did we know for sure that this child was not being kidnapped? Was he transferring her to New York without the knowledge of his wife? Dad thought of more reasons, and with each one, I became a little more skeptical of Dr. Philip Edwards. But I agreed to visit the home of this gentleman, meet his wife and child, and then make a more informed decision. Dad said he would accompany me, but I was able to wiggle out of that arrangement, and he agreed that I could take a trusted friend.

When Dr. Edwards called the next day, I gave him these stipulations, and he said he would call back. Sure enough, I had an invitation to dinner, and my friend and I boarded a bus the very next day. It never occurred to me that a woman who was about to deliver a child and who was caring for a seventeen-month-old might find it difficult to entertain two strangers and serve them a meal. I was more concerned about getting the approval of my parents. Time was of the essence now, for the birth was expected any day, and it was getting close to the weekend when I would be available to take the child to New York.

On arriving at the apartment of the Edwards' we were greeted by Mrs. Edwards, whose whiteness startled me for a moment. She was stunningly beautiful, with shiny black hair to her shoulders. Her Wedgewood warm blue eyes and her peaches- and-cream complexion completed the picture of sweetness and innocence. And then she smiled, and we knew we had come to the right place. I had heard that a pregnant woman dons a glow, and Mrs. Edwards proved the principle. She was the picture of contentment and tranquility that I am now sure belied the true facts. The little girl was mulatto, with brown curly hair, dark brown eyes, and the same shy look of her Dad. She seemed surprised at company arriving, and then became tickled pink to enjoy herself and the attention we provided.

We shared a delicious meal, and as we sat with tea in the living room, Mrs. Edwards explained why she had no relatives or friends to help with her situation. She came from a socially prominent family in Victoria, B.C. When she announced that she would marry Dr. Philip Edwards, a black man, the family cut all ties with her. There was no one to assist her in this emergency or any other. The neighbors and wives of Philip's colleagues simply ignored the couple, unable to tolerate marriage of mixed colour. Dr. Edwards' relatives in the Unites States treated the marriage in the same fashion as their white brethren. My friend and I were enthralled with this love story, and charmed by our newfound friends.

Back in the office the next day, I chose the travel date, and watched the booking chart very carefully, as I travelled on a space-available basis. The flight stayed available up until the time of travel, and I arrived at the airport before Dr. Edwards. The airport agents were my co-workers, and I explained to them why I was taking a baby to New York, for her name had to appear on the manifest. Dr. Phil's eyes watered as he said good-bye to his daughter, but she was having the time of her life, enjoying the attention I was happy to bestow on her, for her sweetness was endearing.

We had several male personnel at the airport, and they were fond of playing jokes on us when we travelled. At that time, our aircraft landed in Burlington, Vermont, for customs and immigration. Unbeknownst to me, the boys at the airport had   sent a message to our Burlington agent to advise customs to be on the lookout for agent Braceland (me) and black baggage. How racist that sounds today, but they considered it as just a practical joke on me. When I opened my bag for inspection, everything had been tied in knots, the work of the agents in Montreal. I still wonder why they thought this to be so funny. The customs inspector knew these agents, and agreed with me that they were immature at best. I was forced to untie everything, while holding the baby, as customs did a thorough inspection. I was then accosted by immigration, and had to prove my way out of carrying another person's child to the United States. Customs and immigration officers whom I knew quite well immediately changed their attitude to me because of this little child. Vermont customs and immigration had always been considered a "country bumpkin" operation, and I later thought that they were proving themselves as "big city" operators, overlooking nothing that could later cause them embarrassment. I endured my discomfort with as much graciousness as I could muster, for there was little I could do, as I would need their help in future airline transactions.

With no further incidents, we re-boarded the aircraft, and immediately upon the aircraft's ascent, the little girl began to scream bloody murder. The pressure was hurting her ears, and this can be extremely painful. All I could do was hold and rock her, singing the few children's ditties I knew.

Our airline did not have flying rights directly between Montreal and New York. We had Montreal-Boston and also Boston-New York, and so it was necessary to change planes in Boston. I entered the terminal, carrying the baby on my shoulder. She was a darling sight in her little dress and matching poke bonnet. I had worked in this terminal, so knew almost everyone. I was met by a black porter, who said, "Miss Braceland, I didn't know you were married." I turned around to show him the baby and was about to say, "I'm carrying the baby for a passenger, Harry." He took one look at the mulatto child and said, "You best just turn around, now. Don't enter the lounge — you won't be welcome." I thought, How foolish — everyone knows me, but said, "Thanks, Harry, that's probably good advice," and kept walking toward the lounge.

On entering the room I encountered a stewardess I had known when I had worked in Boston. She greeted me from across the room with, "Aggie, how great to see you. So you're married now! Let's see that baby." As I turned around, she discovered "that baby" was not pure white, said, "Disgusting," and walked away. I knew then the meaning of discrimination. If that had been my baby, I could not have survived in either the white or black community. I remembered that as I had sat with my crying baby, letting passengers disembark before us, a woman, passing our seat, had said to her husband, "What a disaster, and she's so blond." I had paid no attention, but the remark flew back into my consciousness, and I immediately knew and felt the anguish of Dr. and Mrs. Phil Edwards. And our poor little baby — how would she play the hand she had been dealt? How would she deal with snide remarks, innuendoes and insults? My heart was broken. I had learned firsthand about an ugliness of which I had been completely ignorant. I did not like it, but was too caught up in my own orderly world to ask how I might go about righting this wrong. I remembered this incident when I was bringing up my own children, and hope now that something of my feelings stuck with them.

On arrival in New York, we were met by Dr. Phil's sister, a lawyer, somewhat shy and cool like her brother, but obviously happy to see this child for the first time. She expressed her thanks to me, and invited me to stay the night with her in New York. I declined, saying I had already booked into our house in Flushing and would stay with the stewardess I had roomed with when I lived in Boston. I had no such plans at the time, but I could not bring myself to accept this kind offer, for something had changed. I was now aware of the criticism I might suffer should I accept such an invitation. I had to come to terms with my feelings, and it would take some time for me to recognize that I should do what I think is right, regardless of what people might think or say. Actually, staying with Dr. Phil's sister was not a choice between defying the system and going along with it. I think I just wanted to get away from the whole situation, and wasn't ready to test my righteousness at that particular moment.

Mrs. Edwards had a little boy, and my friend and I went to see her in the hospital. It was the only time I did not ask to see a newborn baby. After the experience I had had, I was afraid she would think I just wanted to see what colour the child was.

[Dr. Edwards had been born in British Guyana, attended New York University and then McGill University Medical School. After his track and field days were over, he joined the staff of Royal Victoria Hospital, where he became an expert in tropical diseases and went on many international medical missions. Heart problems would cause his death in 1971.]

PEACHES

Standing at my counter at Northeast Airlines checking in twenty-one passengers for the evening flight to Boston, I was momentarily distracted as I caught in my peripheral vision, a *real* vision, an unbelievable sight approaching. I presumed she was about to enter the Piccadilly Lounge next door, but was wrong, she was heading my way. She was dressed in a long black sheath, almost touching her toes, which was the fashion at the time. The dress no doubt was poured onto her, but the effect was somewhat softened by the black, tight-fitting jacket that was open.

She wended her way through the Mount Royal lobby, stiletto heels clicking her progress with every step. All heads turned to catch a glimpse of this tall Jean Harlow look-alike. She knew this and did all but bow to the audience, at the prospect of which I feared she would fall out of her clothing. My passengers were enthralled and made a pathway for her to my counter so they could get a better view of this wonder. I stood face to face with her and was fascinated by the huge eyes, ringed with black eyeliner, and eyelashes that seemed to stretch from her eyes down over her multiple strands of pearls of every color, shape and texture. She blinked the eyelashes frequently as she announced her intention of checking in on our flight. When she leaned down to put her baggage on the scale, every head bowed following the line of her body, and hope reigned supreme that the jacket would open and reveal more of her treasures. She spoke in a soft little voice, and I thought the voice didn't match the body, nor the body language, which said, "Here I am, admire me."

After the limousine had departed for the airport, I called in the manifest to the airport agent, advising him of the names, citizenship, weight, baggage information, and other pertinent information. As usual, I alerted my partner on the other end of the phone, as to any unusual or interesting characters. I told Bobby Walcott about the treasure aboard, for he no doubt would want to be on the welcoming committee. After the flight left, Bobby called and said, "Do you know who the woman is?" I admitted that we had never carried her before and I was ignorant of the significance of her travel with our airline. He informed me that she was "Peaches," the much-acclaimed stripper at the Gayety Theatre. How was I to have known that? The airport agents seem to find this amusing, and from then on my nickname was "Peaches."

Many years passed, about forty-five in fact, during which Bobby had become vice president of Eastern Airlines in Miami. After my marriage, and the advent of my family, I had lost touch with most of my co-workers at the airline but heard about their careers.

At this time I was responsible for the operation and profits of nine offices in Quebec and the Atlantic Provinces, and was with the largest travel agency in Canada. One of my managers approached me with a request for help in clearing six seats to Puerto Rico at Christmas. This was an almost impossible task at the time, as all airlines were sold out in October and would not even accept waiting lists. I told her to leave it with me and I would get back to her.

Not having spoken to Bobby Walcott in almost a half-century, I picked up the phone and called his office in Miami. His secretary was most protective of him, screening all calls, and I knew that mine would be put on the back burner. When she asked me who was calling, I said, "Just tell Mr. Walcott that 'Peaches' is on the line." She gathered in her breath, not knowing exactly how to handle this. I sensed that she feared I might be a blackmailer, and had better inform Mr. Walcott. The phone was immediately picked up by Mr. Walcott, with a shout of "Peaches! How many seats do you need?" I said, "Bobby, how did you know that I was in a jam?" "Well," replied Bobby, "after forty-some years, you're not calling me to tell me how good-looking I am." We chatted about the good times we had had in those days, and how the industry had changed. He asked me what flights I needed, and confirmed them immediately. I was glad I had met "Peaches" for she had unknowingly been instrumental in my being able to help someone else who depended on me. We later carried Lili St. Cyr of Bellevue Casino fame, but I was prepared for her and her need for attention.

Thanks, Peaches, wherever you are.

THE RESTAURANT BUSINESS

Mr. Keene, a regular passenger who flew in every week, called me from Boston every Monday to arrange his hotel and limousines for the week. On one of his regular calls, he asked if I could have a meeting with him on his next trip to Montreal. He was general manager for a family-owned restaurant chain in Boston, and was opening a second restaurant in Montreal. It was to be an up-scale eatery on Ste. Catherine Street. He was looking for a personnel manager to hire the help and run a personnel office from a McGill Street location and offered me the job. I would earn much more than I was receiving from the airline, and have a great deal of responsibility. It sounded interesting, and I told him I would like to hear more about it. He arranged for the owners and their wives to meet me in Montreal, and they took me to dinner at a posh restaurant, "Au Lutin Qui Bouffe."   While preparing for their arrival on our flight, I closed the ticket counter and went to apply a fresh coat of paint to my face, leaving my coat and hat in the office, as usual. I had bought a beautiful black coat and a smashing black hat for the occasion, and felt I looked like a very efficient businesswoman in the outfit. When I returned from the ladies' room, both the hat and coat were gone. It was a rather cold evening, and I had nothing to wear over my uniform. Mrs. Keene outfitted me with a jacket she had brought, and off we went in a limousine to the restaurant. The job was explained in detail, and I was most impressed with the respect and courtesy the brothers and their wives had for each other and for Mr. Keene and his wife. I told them I would give them an answer within a week, although I knew then that I would accept the job. Looking back, I think I was most taken with the job title, "Director of Personnel," and the fact that I would need a briefcase for my trips between stores. I would look the part with the briefcase in tow.

I started work on McGill Street, and found that I would also be responsible for the two women who worked in the office. They were nieces of the owners, and were very resentful of my appointment. They treated me with disdain and made life extremely difficult, a fact I did not disclose to my new bosses in Boston. The girls were supposed to show me the payroll system, but refused to do so. I ended up figuring it out myself, and always wondering if I was doing it correctly. It seemed to add up, though, and I plugged along in the dark for the whole time I had the job. I hated every minute I spent in that office; after several months I stopped trying to please the girls and simply did my work. I think this approach irked them even more, for they realized they could not get my goat, and the owners seemed to think I was doing a good job. How I hated that job, and wondered why I had ever accepted it. There were some good days, however, when I had to choose uniforms for the hostesses and waitresses, choose finishing touches for the restaurant, and hire the best people I could find. Each payday, I carried the money for everyone in the restaurant — in the leather briefcase! The people in the restaurant were always glad to see me and treated me with great respect, which lifted my spirits. Of course I always wondered if it was only the money I dispersed that made me so popular!

I learned a lot in the restaurant field, which was completely different from anything I had done before, but most of all I learned that the two women with whom I worked were basically unhappy, and I was the straw breaking the camel's back. They didn't know how to get out of their situation by talking to the management or changing jobs, but took out their frustration on an innocent person. Throughout my career I have met more of this type of person, and because of my experience, have been able to steer away from hiring anyone who seemed to have a grudge against life. I knew that his or her personality had been formed, and would be detrimental to harmony in any office I would run. I was very fortunate to have learned this lesson very early and it saved me from disaster on many an occasion. Oh, I made errors of judgement when choosing personnel, but hiring this type of person is not in my repertoire of mistakes. So I know now that all was not lost, even though at the time I felt I had failed. During my tenure as personnel director, several incidents occurred that probably prompted my employers to be greatly relieved when I tendered my resignation.

The manager of our new upscale restaurant on Ste. Catherine Street, at the corner of Drummond, called me to ask for a meeting. His problem was that the chef was drinking heavily and could not control it. I asked if the chef arrived for his shift under the influence, and he said, "No, that's not the case. He's cold sober then, but becomes intoxicated quickly, getting drunker by the minute." We discussed the pros and cons of the problem, and came to the conclusion that we would have to find his hiding place for the booze. I searched every kitchen cupboard and drawer, then moved on to containers for cooked food. They were deep steel bowls fitting into specially designed spaces. They contained all kinds of hot foods, so I avoided them at first. But some contained sauces and salads, and so, rolling up my right sleeve, I began digging my arm up to the elbow into all sorts of cold foods, feeling around for the offending bottle. After about four or five digs, I found the prize, embedded in the potato salad. The chef was fired that day, but only after he finished his shift! As to the foods I had played around in, I did not ask for any details.

One day, a man approached me in my office, waving a "Deaf and Dumb" sign, asking for a donation to his welfare, so I wrote a cheque for $2 along with a note telling him to go across the street to the Royal Bank, give them the cheque and they would give him $2. A few minutes later — bank lineups weren't as long then — the bank called me to say they couldn't cash the cheque because he had no identification. The bank teller went on to say that when they informed the young man of this fact, he cursed them all out in a profanity not often heard in their establishment. I told her to send him back to me with the cheque and I would put things right for him. When he came back, I asked him to surrender the cheque, which he did begrudgingly. I told him that had he asked me for a job, I could have helped him. If he had said he was hungry, I would have fed him in exchange for work in our restaurant. He came close to hitting me, he was so very angry to have lost his $2 and perhaps his pride. Today I would not risk offending this type of stranger, for fear of becoming a victim.

Mr. Keene of the head office, in one of our telephone conversations, advised me that I should not hire any "rubby-dubs." I informed our managers that there was a hold on hiring more dishwashers for the time being. Our new store manager kept calling me and begging for more help in the dishwashing category and I kept refusing. Several meetings later, I told Mr. Keene that we really were in need of dishwashers, and my new manager was getting very impatient with me. "Well, hire them," was Mr. Keene's reply. "Mr. Keene, you told me *not* to hire any rubby-dubs." "Miss Braceland, what, in your opinion, is a rubby-dub?" "A dishwasher, of course, Mr. Keene." "A rubby-dub, my dear, is a loose term for a wino, or someone who lives by the bottle. They work for a day to get enough money for a drink and are never seen again. That is what I meant. You must be careful not to hire any of these people who prey on restaurants for jobs they never intend to work at." With that, he picked up my phone and called the partners in Boston telling them the story, which he thought was hilarious. I was very embarrassed, for this *naiveté* hardly went with my job of personnel director.

Once a week I would prepare the payroll and head off to the bank to get the proper cash for each pay envelope for the staff. I would put everything in my new leather briefcase, hail a cab, and look forward to the smiles on the faces of the employees, for they knew what I was carrying — their livelihood. One Friday I completed all my tasks, hailed the cab, and arrived at the restaurant, only to discover that I had left the briefcase in the taxi. For a moment I stood facing the manager, and could barely say, "Good Afternoon." I managed to say, "I'm running a little late today, so give me about an hour. I'll be in my office." My legs were like stilts, with no connection to the rest of my body. I wondered how I would be able to climb the stairs to my office, for I was weak, and scared to death. I didn't even remember what taxi company I had used. The thought came to me, *This* is why people commit suicide. How would I be able to replace this money that belonged to hard-working people, some of whom were sole supporters of families, and who depended on their weekly envelope as their only income. I knew that no matter how hopeless the situation, I had to try to find that briefcase.

I called every taxi company, telling them I was having an important meeting and had left my presentation in their taxi. I told them where I had hailed the cab, and left my number, not expecting to hear from anyone. I called Dad next and told him the story. At that moment, I didn't need a lecture, and no one could help me out of this situation, so I didn't need suggestions either. Fortunately, Dad sensed exactly how I felt, and simply said, "Sometimes we make mistakes. That's human. It's how we handle them that makes the difference." I waited some time for return calls from the taxi companies, but received none. My plan was to go to the bank, ask for a loan of the lost amount, not telling them that I had been so careless. First I would have to talk to the manager, explaining that the pay would be late that week, and prepared myself for the agony of just getting out the words. How cruel it would sound.

As I willed myself down that flight of stairs, I heard my telephone ringing, and found that my legs had wings. Perhaps, perhaps. It was the Diamond Taxi Company calling to say they had found my briefcase. It was a call I hadn't really expected. I dared not ask them to check the contents, for I feared they would say it was empty. They said their cab would drop it off to me in a few minutes, and I waited outside, generous tip in hand. I quickly opened the metal clasp, drove my hand into the briefcase, and felt the envelopes thick with dollars and change. I knew I had been rescued, and only then did I offer up a silent prayer. In my desolation, I had forgotten to ask for help from above, but at the moment of my rescue, I thought that God had known all along what a jam I was in and also knew why I hadn't asked Him for help. I wasn't thinking straight and He wouldn't hold that against me. He helped me anyway, or was it those waiters and waitresses, cooks and dishwashers who had said a prayer when they saw me without my briefcase....

A SHORT HOLIDAY

No, the restaurant business was not for me, and it was a relief when I made the decision to resign and return to airline work. I had been interviewed by Trans Canada, and was assured of a passenger-agent position, where I would divide my time between the airline terminal building on Dorchester and University Streets, and the Mount Royal Hotel, my old friend. I would take a short holiday, awaiting the opening of the position at Trans Canada Airlines. Two friends and I decided to drive to Boston for a few days – in the middle of February. My friend's parents were in Florida, and so Valerie had the family Packard. A female friend of Valerie's parents rode with us as far as Concord, New Hampshire. Although to us she was old, she was probably in her fifties. Not interested in our conversation, she remained rather quiet throughout the drive. Each time, however, that Valerie seemed destined for an accident, and this was rather frequently as Val liked to watch the passing scenery as well as join in on any discussions taking place on the long drive, our passenger would shout "My Jesus — wept," flinging her knitting on the car floor. After a few of these outbursts, we became fascinated by her behavior, and Valerie tried to create as many opportunities as possible to witness what we considered the best show on the highway.

After dropping off our passenger, we continued on to Boston, finally pulling up to the main entrance of the YWCA. We had a beautiful room, attractively furnished with overstuffed chairs covered in bright and cheery floral patterns to match the bedspreads. A large bay window allowed the sun to flood the room, at certain times falling on the highly polished dresser and night tables. It was cozy and would suit us fine.

We planned to have a short rest, a bath, and a face overhaul in that order, after which we would change into our going-to-dinner outfits. After about ten minutes of rest, the telephone rang, and we were asked the license number of our car. This being Val's department, she took the call and was advised that we were in a No Parking zone, and would have to move the car immediately. This would take the skills of all three in our trio, so off we went. Guarding our car was a burly Irish cop, with "No Nonsense" written all over his weather-worn map of a face. He complained loudly about the "Damn Canadians not knowing a No Parking sign from a carton of Camels." Val said not a word as we three piled into the car, and Val took off – right through a red light. The cop's whistle summoned us back to his side, and he wryly complimented her on her ability to back up as well as go forward. His own wit seemed to enthrall him. Beginning to laugh hysterically, he waved us on, as Val thanked him for his kindness. I admired her cool.

After several days in Boston, shopping, sightseeing, and dining out every evening, our resources were soon almost depleted. I remembered that American Airlines was on strike, and Northeast Airlines would be overburdened with the overflow traffic. As I had previously worked in Boston, I knew the ropes. Going over to the Copley-Plaza Hotel where Northeast had an office, I checked out the situation. They were delighted to see me, as it was bodies they needed, especially an old hand like myself. I had only one special request. I would have to be paid on a per diem basis, leaving with the cash every day, so that our great lifestyle would not be interrupted or, perish the thought, we should have to return home. Working for the airline would be much more fun than any museum visits or shopping spree I could think of.

All good things finally come to an end, and we packed our clothes, newly bought treasures and mementos for our family and friends, and headed for home in the Packard. Somewhere in Vermont, in the middle of a snowstorm, we hit a skunk and veered off the road into a great immovable wall of a snowbank. We were completely surrounded by snow, with not a hope of getting the car out. It was about ten o'clock at night, late for three young ladies to be snowbound with no hope of discovery or aid.

After about thirty minutes of praying for a miracle, we saw a middle-aged man approaching us. We knew we were finished, and aloud we prayed that God would protect us from a fate worse than death. On reaching our car, the man gestured for me to open my window. I pretended to be deaf and blind, while checking to make sure the door was securely locked. He then began to yell at us, "Do you want help or don't you?" We had a short conference, all agreeing that it would be better to accept his help, and if it turned out that it was not help he was offering, then we could all jump him and strangle him with our prayer beads.

The man turned out to be a fine example of a Good Samaritan. He was able single-handedly to get us out of the snowbank, and we all felt guilty about having doubted his good intentions. Actually, he said he didn't blame us for being extra careful. Little did he know of the fate we had ordained for him, had he tried anything. After the first hurdle had been overcome, we then had to deal with the skunk odor that permeated the car. There was nothing we could have done then, but we made up for our inactivity by worrying about the consequences when Val's parents would return from Florida, especially when they discovered that the driver's door had been ripped off by a taxi. Oh yes, on our second day in Boston, Val had stopped and opened the door to the oncoming traffic. We had the car repaired at a garage that we believe used Stickem's glue to get the door re-attached to the frame, but their price suited our budget at the time.

My problem was that I was wearing a fur coat, my only good winter coat. The following morning, I was scheduled to meet with Trans Canada to arrange details regarding the position they had offered me. I put my odoriferous coat outside for the night, but that did not help the situation. I called Trans Canada and cancelled my appointment. My future boss, Warren Scrivner, said, "Well, Aggie, I've heard all the excuses in the world for people being late or not showing up, but I've never heard this one before. You are either very truthful or very creative, and we can use both of those qualities here at Trans Canada Airlines." I hastened to tell him that I would have a coat by tomorrow, even if I had to buy a new one, and we set up a new appointment. The job was to start as soon as I was ready.

TRANS CANADA AIRLINES

I had been promised a position on the ticket counter as a "passenger agent," however my boss told me that in order for me to get there, I would have to spend a little time in their reservations office, in order that certain protocols be observed. This office was in the bowels of the Canadian National Central Station, and was known to the employees as the "Snake Pit." Fortunately, I was not privy to that information before I accepted the job. We worked eight-hour shifts around the clock. The midnight shift was a dreaded one for me, as I had never before worked through the night. There was only a handful of phone calls, and most of our time was spent trying to stay awake long enough to prepare charts for the following day. Early morning could be a busy time if weather was closing in, as we would have to alert all passengers that flights had been delayed or cancelled. In those days, customer service was all-important. Can any one of us recall now the last time an airline called to say that our flight would be delayed or had been cancelled? Many mornings I prayed for bad weather to make my job a little more interesting.

Some agents found it amusing to place crank calls to their colleagues, putting them through their paces with difficult routings, fare constructions, and generally making a nuisance of themselves in disguised voices. I practiced this once or twice, and to tell the truth it was amusing to watch the other agent put the call on hold, and then in a loud voice say what he or she would really like to say to the caller. The more experienced night shift workers would usually recognize the voice however and just say, "You again, Tommy? Why don't you go back to sleep and give me a rest."

Within several weeks I was transferred to the counter at the Airlines Terminal Building, as agreed, and there I met an old friend from Colonial Airlines, Frankie O'Brien, the Vivian Leigh look-alike with the wonderful personality. Also on the counter was Beatrice Allison, who had gone to school with my sister Rita. Everyone depended on her for the last word in airline fares and routings and I cannot recall one instance when her judgement was ever questioned or was incorrect. How fortunate I was to have these two ladies to count on for assistance if needed. They were the best in our business, and I felt that Trans Canada was indeed lucky to have such good people handling their passengers. Neither one took herself seriously, and both had a marvellous sense of humour, which could make a comedy out of any tragedy. There were other fine people with whom I worked, and I truly enjoyed being part of this team.

I particularly looked forward to the days on which I worked at the Trans Canada counter in the Mount Royal Hotel, my old stomping grounds, where I knew all the hotel counter staff, the bellboys, porters, banquet staff, and managers of various departments. When my passengers called me to obtain a room for them, it was never a problem, even though the hotel was always "fully booked." If our passengers needed American money in a hurry, I could always get the hotel to provide it in non-banking hours. Similarly if any hotel staffers needed airline space, it was a foregone conclusion that I would clear it, even if it took a little time. And close by, at the corner of Peel and Ste. Catherine Streets, ready to assist in any way possible was my old friend Jockey Fleming. I had missed him.

I remember well a gentleman who came to my counter to reconfirm his onward space to Vancouver but we had no record of his reservation. He said that while I looked into this "Air Canada error," he would check into the hotel. He came back like a tiger on the attack, saying that not only did we not have any record of him, neither did the hotel. "Damn Prairie Town" and "Little League Operation," were his comments. I said, " Sir, you mentioned 'Prairie Town.' Do you realize you are in Montreal?" At that moment, choice words began to fly, as did his mighty paws, just missing me as I ducked their onslaught. The ticket counter separated us and, by chance, standing behind our hero was the hotel detective, waiting to calm down my passenger if such action was needed.

Our feisty passenger actually thought he was in Winnipeg, having boarded the wrong flight in Toronto. On arrival here, he used the limousine service, and got off at the first stop, believing it to be the Fort Garry Hotel in Winnipeg. I was not able to get him to Winnipeg that evening as there was nothing operating, but was more than happy to clear a seat on the first flight the next day. At dawn he was on his way, after what I presume was a good night's sleep in the "sold out" Mount Royal Hotel. He was one of the first people who neglected to thank me for my efforts in clearing a hotel room!

BLIND DATE

At Trans Canada, my life was fairly tranquil as the airline had enough personnel so that there was always someone to fill in during the absence of an employee for any reason. Overtime was unusual, and as the ticket counter was open at the terminal from 9-6 and at the hotel from 9-9, and closed on weekends, our social lives took a turn for the better. My friend Val, who was going out with Dennis Fraser, a McGill medical student, asked me if I would go on a blind date with one of Dennis' friends. I accepted, and my date turned out to be very interesting. He was also a McGill student, in chemical engineering. We went to the

Saturday night dance at the Ritz where Blake Sewell's orchestra was the usual band. My friend Frank Monahan was the pianist with Johnny Holmes' band at Victoria Hall, and though I had been there before, I had not been to the Ritz on a Saturday night. I felt right at home, as the formats were similar. The surroundings however were more opulent, for nothing can compare to the atmosphere of the Ritz Hotel.

My date was Gordon Henchey, a tall, handsome, clean-cut, young man, whom I judged to be about two or three years younger than I. His boyish face belied his high level of intelligence that I was to discover as I got to know him better. He was quiet and unassuming, with an effortless British sense of humor. I liked his naturalness. We continued to see each other, and it was only after I bought a camel hair coat and saddle shoes, in order to look more collegial, that I realized I was more interested in Gordon Henchey than I had cared to admit.

At the beginning of December, I refused a date for New Year's Eve, presuming I would be going out with Gordie. I was shocked when he told me that he was going up north with his brother for New Year's weekend. I decided that if anyone invited me out I would accept. Before Christmas, I met a really nice young man who asked me to go to a private party with him. I accepted, thinking even if he were Dracula, I would accept. I hoped Gordie would get wind of the fact that I did not stay home waiting for him. When he phoned me, I was prepared to say, "New Year's Eve? Oh, yes, I had a marvellous time," but he didn't ask. I did inquire about his weekend, saying that I hoped it was a sparkling one with his brother. It was. No details were asked for nor given by either of us.

As for the party, my date and I got along very well, until he disappeared just before midnight. I excused myself from the festivities, and headed for the upstairs bathroom. As I got to the top step, there in front of me was my friend, kissing some girl I hadn't seen before. He saw me out of the corner of his eye as I turned around and headed downstairs. I called a cab, which took some time in coming. My date said he wanted to explain, but I was not interested in hearing from him. Finally my taxi came, and I fled home into the arms of my parents, who wondered why I was home before midnight. I told them what had happened, as I struggled to keep the tears from my eyes and my voice.

In the new year, I had a call from this young man, asking if I would go out for a drink with him so he could explain. I thought it was only fair to give him the opportunity. We went to Ruby Foo's on Decarie Boulevard. He explained that the girl I saw was the girl he had hoped to marry. They had had a serious disagreement, ending their engagement. He had asked me out to hurt her feelings, but when they saw each other at the party, they both knew they had made a big mistake. What could I say? After all, I had only gone out with Ian to make Gordie realize I would never sit home alone if he preferred going out with his brother instead of me. Yes, I think I was growing fond of Mr. Gordon Henchey. The more I got to know him, the more I realized what high ideals he possessed. I admired his standards, his ethics, his sense of fair play, and his logical mind. He could be objective in the most subjective circumstances, making unemotional decisions based on fact and fairness. Opposites do attract. I am more emotional, make quick decisions (sometimes regretted) and find it difficult to be objective when a family member or close friend is concerned. Yes, I think we were fairly well suited. Time would tell.

VANCOUVER

Shortly after Dad's death, I decided to use one of my passes to take Mum to Vancouver to visit my sister Phyllis. Although mother was only sixty-six years old at the time, in those days we considered this to be a very old age. I felt responsible for her. Our flight made several stops en route to Vancouver. As we were on a space-available basis, we were very lucky we were not deplaned in some remote prairie town. We reached Vancouver without incident, and checked into the Sylvia Hotel, quite close to the convent Phyllis called home. On calling her, she was most disappointed that we were in a hotel, as arrangements had been made for us to stay in the convent. The sisters had changed the infirmary into a twin-bedded room for us. We couldn't refuse my sister Phyllis, and arrived at the convent minutes later.

I remember the three-inch heels on my alligator shoes. On the highly polished floor, I found it nearly impossible to navigate. My sister found a pair of black walking shoes that certainly did the job of securely attaching me to the floor, but didn't do much for my image, I thought. We visited some of my parents' friends who had moved to Vancouver.

77

We saw Stanley Park, several museums, shopped, and talked for many hours with my sister, who had not been home during Dad's illness. Every moment of his life was relived and passed on to her. She was hungry for every detail we could recall, and in the retelling, we seemed to address our grief and lessen our sorrow. We began a healing process then and there.

Sadly, our visit came to an end, and we headed for the Vancouver Airport. We were told that we might be off-loaded at any one of the stops en route to Montreal, as it was a very busy time. We didn't even make it out of Vancouver. Not wanting to burden my sister with this news, we checked into the Hotel Vancouver. We went to the airport for every flight, but always came back to the hotel, having had no luck. After several days of staying at a posh hotel, with round-trip transportation to the airport on many occasions, my resources were growing thin. I was treating Mum to this trip, so said nothing to her of my predicament. I downgraded our accommodations to the Georgia Hotel, and hoped for the best.

Three days after our original date, we were able to board a flight to Montreal. On arrival in Calgary, we were bumped, and at this point I had run out of money. I didn't even have the limousine fare to town. On debarking from the aircraft, I found a chair for Mum, placed her book, *The Robe*, firmly in her hands, and headed for the baggage arrival. While awaiting our baggage, I looked around at the other passengers. One older gentleman was quite friendly to me, and asked if I was going into town. I replied that I was, and he offered to give me a drive in the private limousine he had ordered. I accepted his offer, gushing, batting my eyelashes, saying that I would be going to the Palliser Hotel. He gave me a big smile, saying, "Why, that's where I'm headed." I could almost see this thoughts, This dame is even easier than I thought. He insisted on carrying the baggage to the limousine departure area.

In the meantime, I ran over to Mum, telling her she would have to walk a little more quickly than usual. I took her to the limousine and said to the man, "My mother is so very grateful to you, aren't you, Mum?" I felt like a cheat. Mum really didn't get it. She had no idea why she should be grateful to this stranger, nor why we were riding with him, when the regular limousine had always served our purpose. No conversation ensued, my hero being so angry he didn't trust himself to speak. I was angry, also, but at myself for playing this role. Because I was the host of this trip, I would not let myself ask Mum for money, even though I knew that she at least had enough in her purse for the limousine.

After checking in at the Palliser Hotel, I knew I would have to do some fancy footwork in order to be able to stay there until a flight was available. I had used my savings for this trip, such as they were, and hadn't planned for this contingency. Shades of Boston crossed my mind. Yes, the Boston Caper could be used here.

Seeing that Mum was engrossed in her book, I headed down to the Trans Canada counter in the Palliser. They were very busy, and I asked the manager if he needed some help. He was relieved to know that I had both reservation and ticket counter experience, and offered me a verbal contract for as long as I needed to work. I was able to check the space availability hour by hour, and after two days, the flights opened up, and again we headed for the airport. My earnings covered our hotel bill, including meals, with a little left over for travelling.

Finally we reached Dorval Airport. If I ever had to choose a travelling companion, I would want that person to be a replica of Mum. She never questioned my reasons for doing what I did, enjoyed herself in a quiet way and, thank God, was an avid reader who was content to be left alone with her book while I found solutions to our problems. Some fifty years later, I was having a conversation with Father Peter Sabbath when he was an assistant to Father Tom McEntee, pastor of St. Edmund's Catholic Church in Beaconsfield. I asked him what had been influential in interesting him in Christianity, having been exposed only to Judaism. He said that as a small boy, his mother had taken him to a movie, which was his introduction to the life of Christians. That movie was *The Robe*. The face of my mother, head bowed, contentedly reading her book crossed my consciousness, and I thanked her silently for those few days together. Who says she didn't have an inkling of what was happening?

MR. READ

It was the summer of 1951, five minutes before the six o'clock closing of our Trans Canada Airlines office in the International Terminal at University Street and Dorchester Avenue (now René Lévèsque.) The executive offices were closed, and I was alone in the public office. The door opened, and four harried people weighed down with more baggage than one would expect for ten people staggered forward and dropped their heavy loads at their feet in front of the counter. Obviously they were a family: mother, father and two teenagers. The father, a soft-spoken gentleman but obviously a take-charge person, explained that they had to make their flight to London. It was preparing for take-off in a little more than an hour. This seemed an impossibility, in view of the fact that it was an international flight, and that many steps had to be followed even before they boarded a limousine to the airport. However, I proceeded to get the facts, and learned that the family had been on board the *Franconis,* a Cunard ship bound for England, when a message had been received that Mr. Read was needed *immediately* at The Hague. The shipping company had sent a tender for the passengers and they had disembarked only minutes before, coming by taxi to our office.

When it came time to pay for the tickets, Mr. Reid had no cash. He explained that his services and expenses were to be paid for in England. However, he was prepared to give me his personal cheque — a red flag to me. We were not permitted to accept cheques at that time, and it could well mean your job if you did not go by the rules.

Here was Mr. Read, with his children searching their pockets for any money they could find to help their father. The mother sat within hearing distance, but never uttered a word, and the look of confidence on her face made me wonder if Mr. Read was a master at this kind of chicanery. That was the worst thought I had, but the "Bill" episode had made me wary of every cheque producer. I was unable to verify the steamship story because of the time, and I was working on a deadline with our flight due out in minutes.

Mr. Reid showed me the family passports, and their last name was indeed Read. There were no hints to confirm his story. He reminded me somewhat of my father, and I was sympathetic to him, but still fearful of the loss should I be wrong in my judgement. In one moment I made my decision, called the airport, told them I was adding four passengers, and asked for permission for delay if necessary. I issued the tickets, accepted the cheque, obtained all kinds of information should I need it for Guy Drummond, and the deed was done. For days I lived in fear that I would receive a notice from accounting, each day at six o'clock heaving a sigh of relief that I had been spared. The notice never came. But several months later the following letter was passed on to me.

G.R. McGreglor, Esq.,
President, Trans-Canada Airlines, Montreal, P.Q.

Dear Sir,
I want to thank you indeed for the trouble taken by Trans-Canada to get me to the emergency session of the International Court of Justice, which was held last Saturday to deal with the Anglo-Iranian Oil dispute. I had arrived in Canada by the *Franconis* and reached Montreal at 5.00 p.m. on the Thursday. The last flight that could possibly get me to The Hague for the hearing left at 7.30. At your desk was a most intelligent, obliging and competent young woman, who succeeded in getting me to The Hague in time for the hearing on the Saturday morning. I think that her name was Miss Braceland (I'm sure about the "Brace" part of her name) and I should be much obliged if you would let her know that her efforts were successful and how much they were appreciated by me and by my colleagues.

Yours sincerely,
John E. Read
Mr. Justice J.E. Read
35 Wilton Crescent, Ottawa, Canada

Many questions came to my mind after this episode. Number one was where was the government when it came to providing accommodation to London via my airline, and with the onus on me personally to accept a cheque? Number two was what would the chairman of the board have said in his letter if the cheque had bounced? Would there have been a letter or just a pink slip?

GORDIE

While I was away, I had not spoken to Gordie. Phone calls were very expensive, especially from a hotel. I found that I had missed him, and on arrival home, called him. It was then that we both realized we didn't want to spend time away from each other. We became unofficially engaged, and in May he placed a ring on my finger. We were to be married in September.

All my sisters had had a reception at home. Since I was the only one left, my parents had moved to an apartment, and Dad had since died. I would have to make some preparations for a wedding and a reception. Knowing the people at the Mount Royal Hotel, I dropped in to see Mr. Borbe, the banquet manager. He quizzed me about the type of reception, the number of people and other details. He asked me if I would permit him to handle everything his way. I asked him about the cost of such an arrangement. He said, "Just let me handle it, Miss Braceland, and then when you see what I have done, we can make adjustments or complete changes." So be it. He was possibly the best-known banquet manager in Montreal, with the exception of the one at the Ritz hotel, and so I felt I could trust his judgement.

Several weeks went by, and then I received a call from his secretary asking me to come in to see Mr. Borbe. The menu was more than I had ever dreamed of and he had sketches of what the tables would look like, drawings of the glacéed items that would adorn the serving tables, and a sketch of the head table and one other, even showing flower arrangements of his choosing. This was exactly what I would have chosen, given a runaway budget! I asked Mr. Borbe the cost per person for approximately a hundred guests. His answer, "Our price to you will be $1.00 per person."

I could not believe my good fortune, and asked Mr. Borbe if my ears had betrayed me. He said that over the years I had brought business to the hotel, including the banquet section, and this was the hotel's way of saying Thank you. What a show of class! There was no doubt in my mind as to why I had had such a love affair with the Mount Royal Hotel over the years. They had always handled situations with class, although I had not put a name to it until then. On the day of my wedding and reception at the Mount Royal, the bellboys and porters were lined up in the lobby as we disembarked from our limousine, and entered the hotel. Each and every one offered his good wishes to Gordie and me, and I invited them all in for a drink or a coffee, but they were wiser than to accept, even though Saturday was a slow day for them.

The Mount Royal is no longer a hotel, its vocation now a high-end shopping mall, *Les Cours Mont Royal*, featuring trendy boutiques. I have not wanted to enter, for I wish to maintain my mind's eye view of the old Mount Royal Hotel, and not be distracted by the new and "nouveau" face of Peel Street. I plan to take a day, however, and spend it on Peel Street to see if it could ever have the same appeal. I want to see the spot where A.J. Alexander had their superb fur shop at the front of the hotel, with their display of lush mink coats, sometimes carelessly strewn on the floor, sometimes draped over beautiful mannequins. In front of the mink display was a sign that read *Se Habla Espagnol*. I had gathered enough courage to enter the store at the beginning of my tenure at the Mount Royal. Stepping up to the salesman, I asked to see the *Se Habla Espagnol* fur that was on display.

This particular salesman was an older person, and explained in detail that the furs didn't have individual names, although they were all different, some male, some female, and from different areas, and having different properties. They had different "general" names. For example, the one I liked was a female "Black Diamond." On a short office break, I really didn't care to waste my time with useless information, but listened intently until he came to the part about "and that means 'We speak Spanish here'." He burst out laughing, and so did I. For the rest of the time I spent at the Mount Royal, he and I became friends who always shared a smile or a laugh. Another favorite place was the Vogue Shoe Shop, where they had sizes to match just about any foot. I bought my shoes there until they closed their doors in the 'eighties and since then have found it difficult to find a shop that catered to very long slim feet. Many years later, I shopped for a mink coat, and was careful to ask if it was male or female, and what general category it fitted. But I didn't ask if it spoke Spanish.

And so it came time to tell Trans Canada of my plans to be married, and request a week off for our honeymoon. To my amazement, Trans Canada informed me that women who married were automatically out of a job. That was the rule in those days, and we did not even question why. I parted company with Trans Canada and as a memento of my days with them, they presented me with a beautiful Moorcroft vase, which didn't ease the pain of being jobless, but did help to brighten an almost empty apartment.

My husband, Gordie, had lived most of his life in Quebec City as part of the English community, and during that time he had become fluent in French. He attended an English high school, Boys' High, which followed the British school system. We have just this year given to our grandchildren the last of his many prizes for proficiency, etc., that he received during his time at the high school. Books were the prizes of the day, classics like *David Copperfield, Kim, Alice in Wonderland,* and others that we have encouraged our offspring and theirs to read.

After his graduation as a chemical engineer, Gordie accepted a position at Atlas Asbestos. While at Atlas, Gordie was sent to England for about six weeks. He shopped as much as he was able to, considering our tiny budget, and came home with two beautiful Royal Doulton figurines, "Cissie" and "Miss Demure." When writing to me to let me know that he had purchased these two ladies for me, he called them "Sissy" and "Miss Demeanor," and that is how I will always think of them. His sense of humour is unique and charming.

Upon the birth of our third son, my sister called Gordie at the office to see if the baby had been born. A confrère stated that Gordie was not there, but he believed we had had a boy, as Gordie had flown out of the office, saying, "Another goddamn college education." Another child followed our third son, and we were blessed with a girl. There were no comments about a college education. How our plans, opinions and options changed during the next few years. By the time our daughter was in kindergarten we were already wondering how we would manage her university education.

CARS

The first summer after our wedding was spent at Rawdon, in the Laurentians, with my in-laws at their cottage. Gordie and his father stayed in Montreal during the week and arrived every Friday for the weekend. As their relatives arrived about the same time, having succumbed to the charm of a Laurentian weekend in their own retreats, they would drop over to say hello, and thus would begin the Friday night conversations I was never to forget.

The first subject of conversation was the various routes they had travelled, one saying he came by Route 17, as he deemed it the most scenic, with fewer potholes and less dust. The Provenchers on that route had the best home-baked beans. The next would recount the tale of their journey on Route 37 because he and his family loved that particular scenery and the marvellous road, and in Ste. Julienne one found the best heavy cream in the strawberry season, even though it meant not getting the best butter and eggs in Ste. Calixte. And so it went, through four or five participants with as many different routes and reasons. Not being a driver, I was agog with wonder, and could not fathom so many people being so enthralled with the subject.

The second time it happened, it was deju vu, and I was a sentence ahead of each one, but I was mistaken, for each had changed his route, saying he had chosen it for the very reason he had chosen another route the previous week. No one remembered what the other had said the week before, and so the conversation flowed exactly as it had done before, but with all positions reversed. I remained silent during this conversational blitz, as I had nothing to offer.

To my dismay, when friends came from town for a country visit on a Saturday or Sunday afternoon, they would acknowledge everyone with a warm greeting, such as, "Hello, you look wonderful. We came up by Route 37." The third week when it started, I had the urge to jump in and sing, in the deepest baritone voice I could muster, "I came On the road to Mandalay where the flying fishes play, and the dawn comes up like thunder all across the bay." Perhaps I could accompany this with gestures. Each succeeding week the urge became stronger, and my repertoire enlarged to include, "I hitchhiked, to the tune of 'Going My Way'." Quite a sight that would have been, as I was in my eighth month of pregnancy. I had to resist the temptation, as I wished to maintain my status as "Charming Mute Daughter-in-Law," as was the custom in those days. There were times when I had to leave the room, fearing I would let loose with another of my ridiculous thoughts. I was particularly fond of, "Me? I took the 'A Train'." Eight weeks of routings and I held my ground as a good listener, always retiring to another room to get away from Route 17 and to relegate Mandalay and the other troublemakers to their proper places, as far back as possible in my brain.

When walking to the beach on those lovely weekends, Gordie never questioned why I would suddenly break out in song and dance. I did renditions of "Won't you Come Home, Bill Bailey, Won't you come Home," "Take the scenic One Thirty ni–ine," and belted out other equally stirring ballads. I have never explained to Gordie my sentiments about these conversations, for after all he was then, and remains, a part of them. In later years, I realized that this ritual had been going on, mainly among men, since the automobile was invented. It seemed to be the safest avenue of approach to other more controversial topics, such as who will invade whom and why the Red Sox were not at the top of their game. It honed up the conversational skills, preparing them for other more important parries in the art of conversation.

I have never had an affinity with automobiles or any other type of vehicle. I do not form a friendship with my stove or vacuum, and my car falls into the category of something that does its job, while I do mine. I have never become cozy enough with a car to name it Bessie or Herbert or any other moniker, not even "Bucket of Bolts," which was popular for a while. I am happy if it will get me to my important appointments on time, without grumbling. Those appointments include the butcher and vegetable man in the shopping center. I occasionally drop in to see the pharmacist, to advise him that if he is running short of any prescription drugs, to give us a call, for we have everything on hand. For this, I do not need to know how many horsepower I have, or where the battery is. I leave that in the hands of the people who need this information on a daily basis.

I believe my husband and children are in the above category. When my children visit us, I can usually tell how long it will be before the subject of automobiles comes up. At one time, when they were away at university, returning for a long weekend or holiday, they would become quite revved up as they discussed how long it took to drive home. In each story the time was shorter. At the time, I was not privy to these stories, and I am grateful. One son owned a fifty percent interest in a car, and we were entertained with the stories of that arrangement. Now they discuss the merits of all the cars on the market, the good old cars they have owned, and the clunkers they had bought in their younger, more inexperienced, days, long before they became car experts. They set up marketing plans for General Motors and the Japanese and German companies, and debate the merits of leasing against those of buying outright. I tune out during this time, and take bets with myself on who will have coffee and who will have tea at dinner. I wonder if there is enough strawberry shortcake and if not, perhaps I can slap on a little more whipped cream to make it look respectable. What's that, Peter? Oh yes, my car is in good shape, and I love where the battery is.

I don't recognize different makes of cars, as I pay no attention to them. A few years ago I said, "The Morgans have a lovely new car – how nice for them." Gordie said, "I must have a look." He went outside with a rake in his hand, ostensibly to work in the garden, for we would never want to appear over-interested in the business of our neighbour. In a minute Gordie returned, saying, "Why were you remarking on the Morgan's new car?" Thinking he was complimenting me on being more observant than usual I replied, "Oh, I don't know, I just can't help noticing these things." He replied, " Strange that you should notice it now, because it was their new car two years ago." No, my interest in cars is not very acute.

Recently we drove up north to the cottage that Gordie's parents used to own. I imagined the summer sun falling on the cars in their driveway and in the driveways of their next-door neighbours, their relatives. I could hear the conversation in the living room, and this time I could join in, apologizing for my lack of communication so many years ago. Arriving in Rawdon on a Friday night and joining in on the conversation took experience, not so much in the driving ways of the community, but in the cameraderie and understanding that exists among city folk gone country. It takes some time to develop, and I was not a seasoned traveller. As we sat in our car, we relived those conversations, and wondered how Gordie's parents would feel about the new direct highway, where berries in season are not readily available without leaving the route, and where homemade baked beans are not to be found anywhere.

THE TRAVEL AGENCY

In 1951, the year of our wedding, I had been working for Trans Canada Airlines (now Air Canada). In those days, long before women's liberation, it was understood that women were automatically out of work the day they said "I do." Men however, could marry as many times as they liked (and some of them did) and retain their positions.

Upon "retirement" from the airline, I found myself at loose ends, pondering what I would do with my life. I didn't have to wonder long, for we were presented with four children in six years. For the first few years, we managed without a washer, dryer or dishwasher, household helpers that are considered indispensable today. The children's toys were cardboard boxes that came with the groceries, and made into trains and buses. Dinky toys were treasured, and we managed a few of these on birthdays and at Christmas. Books were essential, for both Gordie and I were avid readers, and believed that books were always good friends to have on hand. A few of them went a long way, as children love to hear the same stories over and over. Our weekly luxury was *Time Magazine*, which we read from cover to cover. In 1957 we built a house in Beaconsfield, where our children played in open fields, discovered frogs and garter snakes, crawfish and toads. These were happy days, though, and there are times when I wish I had a few little ones around, needing a kiss and a hug.

When Betty Ann, our youngest, was three, I was beginning to be restless. Our Beaconsfield neighbours were starting to take a day off every week, to curl in the winter and golf in the summer. I decided that I would like a holiday also, one day a week. That meant doing something I really enjoyed, which wasn't curling or golfing. I began to watch the ads in the local weekly newspaper, *The News and Chronicle*. One Thursday I spotted an ad calling for a sales person. Dialing the number, I was greeted by a voice from the depths of despair. "Memorial Gardens," it said. I was looking for a day out, in a place that could lift my spirits. This was not the place.

Each week, I glanced through the paper, and another ad did catch my eye. It was for a fairly new travel agency wanting someone with my background one day a week. At the interview, I found that the agency was run by a person who had no experience and whose former profession was in the area of adding machines. I felt my ten years of expertise would be helpful and he agreed. I applied for and got the job.

When the owner said he had a beer income and champagne taste, I wondered what brand of beer he liked. After his offer of $13 a day for my services, it seemed likely that he was drinking from the bottom of the barrel. Mum encouraged me to accept the position anyway because it would give me a change of scenery on a regular basis. She offered to mind the children one day a week. I was really grateful to her, and to this day have not forgotten her kindness, for by this time she was in her late seventies. Three of the children were in school, and Betty Anne was a dear little girl who loved her grandmother, so I accepted the offer, hoping it would not be too much for Mum.

I remember receiving my first call, for they put me to work at nine a.m. when I arrived for my first day of work. It was from a Reverend Eddis, who asked me the difference between First Class and Economy to Toronto. My boss had left immediately, giving me no tariffs or any other helpful information. I didn't even know that there were two classes of service. I called Gordie, who was a frequent business traveller. I asked, "What's the difference between First Class and Economy?" he said. "The fare, you dummy," and laughed. I said, "This is really urgent, I'm serious. Please get your Air Canada timetable, as I have a client on the other phone." Gordie told me that Economy was $25 and First Class was $31. I actually kept Reverend Eddis on the line while returning to him saying the line to the agent would be free in a moment, somewhat like the automatic system now in place. Thanks to Gordie I was able to help Reverend Eddis – and he very kindly kept using our services. So much had changed in ten years, but I studied at home, and finally felt competent again.

Not having had any connection with airline business in ten years, and with no experience in the steamship business, I found it somewhat difficult to catch up, but enjoyed studying and familiarizing myself with the travel agency business. When I was working for Colonial Airlines in the forties, I had been sent to the Thomas Cook Agency as "Miss Bermuda" when Colonial was promoting its new service to that destination. During the week I was there, not one person approached me for information on Bermuda or Colonial Airlines, some merely wanting to know if we had a washroom. I hardly considered that experience a helpful addition to my resume. My airline references were helpful though, especially the one from Hank Canvin, the district sales manager for Delta Airlines, previously Northeast Airlines. Hank was well known in the West Island, and had had dealings with the travel agency owner.

All went swimmingly well, and as we grew, the agency hired more part-time workers. Luckily, one of them, Barbara Hare, was an ex-Air Canada employee, whose work ethic paralleled mine. I could hand off my work to her, without a great deal of explanation, and vice versa. We both kept detailed notes on every client and never erased anything so we could go back to the first client meeting knowing everything there was to know about a booking. Sadly this was not the case with other employees. I began to expect emergency phone calls requesting that I come in as soon as possible, the manager saying they were "swamped with business." After a few of these emergencies, I came to understand that something had gone wrong, and needed a fix. On one occasion, I was at home, having been diagnosed with pneumonia. The office called to see how soon I would be coming back. I had been booking two clients to South America, and they didn't know what to do next. They asked if they could send the clients to my home. I actually said yes. I got out of bed, tried to look presentable, and, feeling really ill, handled that couple in our living room. I must have thought myself some kind of martyr.

I found that it was almost impossible to take over someone else's work, inasmuch as there was no detail, no rhyme nor reason as to why they had proceeded as they had. I found that poor connections had been booked due to a lack of experience, and in general, my job was no longer "a fun day out." Barbara and I felt the same way, but when her husband was transferred to Toronto, her problem was solved. I knew that eventually I would have to work almost full time, in order to give the best passenger service to my clients.

Eventually that day came. It meant leaving for the office after the children, fortified by a good breakfast, left for school. I fixed the grapefruit and oatmeal the night before, to give me a head start. I left the office at noon, to be home when the children arrived for lunch, and returned to the office after their departure for school. I worked until three o'clock and was home for them when they arrived from school. I then had lots of time for homework and supper preparation. I loved every minute of the day. I don't recall feeling overworked at home,

90

perhaps because in those days, a working wife was expected to carry on as though there had not been a change in her status. It wasn't common for a wife to work, and husbands permitted this change only if things remained the same as they had been. I didn't even find that odd at the time. It was the way things were. There were days when I had to bring files home to complete, and sometimes this got in the way of the routine. I won't say those days were easy, for I am sure it was frustrating for my family when, on occasion the client seemed to come first. While my family was my first concern, I could not do a less than perfect job for a client, and so sometimes there was a choice to be made. On those rare days, I felt tired.

Later on, I hired a part-time housekeeper, who came in after lunch and tidied the house, doing the ironing and other daily chores. She looked after the children as though they were her own, and every one of my four was completely taken with her. She also started preparation for the dinner, and so I stayed until five o'clock or six if it was a busy day. Dorothy Allan was the name of my new housekeeper, and what a joy she was! She asked me to buy a sewing machine so she could do the mending and the hemming, and would I mind if she designed and made new drapes? Would I? Try me. She noticed that my *Good Housekeeping* recipe book was in tatters, for I couldn't cook anything without that precious book, not having much talent in the kitchen area. She asked to borrow it to copy some recipes. She returned it on my birthday, rebound, with my name engraved on the cover. She made light of it, saying, "It was nothing, as my husband, Jack, is a bookbinder." It was a sad day when, a few years later, the Allans left for British Columbia and I had to find a replacement.

Before Mrs. Allan left, however, she insisted that someone in the household learn to use the sewing machine. Not our daughter, but our son Peter stepped up to the plate. Peter always looked neat, no matter what he was wearing, but being somewhat impatient, he seemed to fear that there would be a delay in the processing of ill-fitting clothes if he did not volunteer his services. Gordie always said that if he wanted to hide something, he would put it in the sewing or mending basket, where I would never find it. Peter worked out an arrangement with Betty Ann. He would do all the hemming if she would do the shirt ironing. I won't comment too much on how this worked out, but I did hear on several occasions that there were many more shirts to iron than hems to turn. I did find a replacement for Dorothy Allan, but never again was I to see such generosity and talent as displayed by this wonderful woman.

TEA AND SYMPHONY

One day my boss asked me if I enjoyed music. I said, "Yes, very much." He then asked me to go to the symphony with him. He had excellent tickets. Things had indeed changed in ten years, during which I had a very tentative relationship with the husbands of my neighbours, tentative inasmuch as we said, "Good Morning" or "Good Evening" and at parties, they were always with my husband as we women gathered to discuss our important matters. So I was not only surprised at this turn of events, but insulted as well, for my boss knew very well that I had a husband and four children. I replied (trying to keep the ice out of my voice, but allowing a little of it to trickle in) that if I were lucky enough to go to the symphony, it would be with my husband. He became enraged, disappeared, and returned with two yellow tickets in his hand. He threw them on my desk and said, "So go with your husband!" I noticed his face was very red, and he was very angry. I thought, There goes my job. I then had to figure out how to work up my husband's enthusiasm, for he was not a particular fan of classical music. On top of that, where would we find an evening babysitter? And what about parking? The cost of the evening would be prohibitive. Gordie was very happy to attend the symphony concert, because it seemed to please me so much. He found the story of my boss quite amusing, and was not a bit jealous, which ticked me off somewhat. We worked our way around the other obstacles, and off we trotted to partake in an evening of pure joy.

As it happened, we were spotted at the symphony concert by neighbours whom we did not know had recognized us. A week later I received a phone call from the neighbour, saying that since we were such avid symphony fans, they were inviting us to an evening of symphony at their home the following Saturday evening. I said I would let her know after I had checked with my husband, whose reply was,

"Once, shame on you for asking me and Twice shame on me, if I agree." But being a really good sport, he said, "Sure, I'll go to your symphony." We walked a block or two to the home of our neighbour. It was a star-filled, clear evening, and we knew this would be a night to remember.

We were ushered to our seats without introduction to the other guests, for the symphony was about to start. Our host informed us that speakers had been installed in every room, as their children were also music lovers. The music started, the silence of the guests was deafening, but the music was loud and clear. There was nothing wrong with the acoustics of that house that a downward turn of a button could not fix, and I wished I had brought some well-hidden earplugs. Most of the enraptured guests had their eyes closed, and a glance at my husband told me that he too was immediately carried away to a serene place, as he sat transfigured, eyes tightly shut — and I thought *I* was the music lover. After a few minutes, I became restless, wanting to escape the boom-tiddi-boom of the base, the whine of the wind instruments and the velocity of the violins, but delivery was not at hand.

For two hours there was not a sound except the loud music, but at ten o'clock mercifully everything stopped. Gordie came to and displayed a small smile, knowing that now finally the drinks would appear. This was not to be. Instead we were served strong lukewarm tea with a social tea biscuit. The cups and saucers were whisked away from us after about one minute so that there would be not a sound when the music began again. There was still not time for introductions. After the strings were strutted out again, silence reigned. Gordie resumed his saint-like attitude, and I tried in vain to do the same. The music was shattering not only my ears, but my nerves as well. I used one hand to hold one leg still, while that leg held the other in place. When would we be relieved of our pain? I thought at one stage we were to have a little recess, but it was only to turn over the cassette, and when one person uttered the words, "How lovely," the hostess raised her eyebrows in severe reprimand. Dear God, how would I survive? I did pray for courage, and for the stamina to keep my legs from jumping like Mexican jumping beans.

There came a time when I knew the jig was up for me, and I would have to excuse myself, but at this exact moment the music stopped, and it was like music to my ears. It was after midnight and we had been sitting like mummies for four hours and fifteen minutes. We thanked our hosts, said goodnight to the strangers, and headed for home. When I was able to put one foot in front of the other, for rigor mortis was well on its way, I thanked God for the opportunity to walk a few blocks in the fresh air.

As the acclaimed music lover, I mentioned nothing of my distress to Gordie, because of his obvious enjoyment. I did say however, "I was so happy to see how much you enjoyed the music tonight." He replied, "What music? I didn't hear a thing. I planned my business trip to the Maritimes for next week, and it saved me from doing it tomorrow. When's the next concert?"

THE OFFICE

Back at the office, I was not only conferring with clients, but was also going out to new companies opening on the West Island, soliciting their business. I was also asked to compose and type most of the letters written by the manager and owner. My own caseload was forty or fifty ongoing files, trips in the planning stage. The workload was severe, and even though I had been given one raise to $16 a day (I wasn't paid for any days off due to illness or any other reason), my housekeeper was doing better financially than I was. I wasn't too bothered by this, for I was completely in love with the work I did and the people I met. Curling and golf could not compete in any way. Not surprising, as I didn't know how to do either.

Finally the company hired a secretary. Her name does not escape me, however, in my mind's eye she was always known to me as "Miss Manipulation." With a beautiful slim figure, age was on her side. At twenty-one, with a lovely face, she had only to smile at our lovesick boss for him to give her anything she requested. I thought that a bit of training might have been a good request for her to make. I had been the fair-haired girl, but all that was forgotten when Miss Manipulation walked into our office. She went through all the letters I had composed, and chose the ones she liked the best. One day she copied one verbatim as usual, addressed it to a client, and left it on her desk. The owner picked it up (as she had intended), read it, and went into raves about her ability in the creative department. He turned to me and said, "And what is your specialty, Mrs. H?" What was this? After being the fair-haired girl who could slay Goliath if asked, was I now relegated to the "has-been" box in favour of a plagiarist? Did I care? Yes, about my reputation, but not about the job. I wasn't even working for a "Champagne" kind of guy. "My specialty, you ask? Date squares!" I replied in a rather loud voice. I then headed for the door, made sure it slammed as I closed it, and went home. I waited for the call telling me that I had been fired. No such call came. I did however hear from the owner, pleading with me not to leave. I wanted him to ask why I was so angry, but he didn't. Another lesson learned: emotional displays are never effective.

Miss M. had an appointment one day with the hairdresser next door to our office. She left without advising anyone where she was going, and hours elapsed before she returned, wearing a huge white towel around her head. She sat down at her desk in the main office, and continued to work as though this was normal attire. A half-hour passed, and the little lady disappeared again, only to re-appear in the same outfit. She departed and returned intermittently for the rest of the afternoon. The staff acted as though we were all blind, and the manager said not a word. That evening I had a call at home from him, apologizing for her behaviour. "No, Mr. X., you should be apologizing for *your* behaviour for allowing this to happen in a respected business office, with clients laughing at our expense. You have well-behaved, dedicated staff who would not even dream of embarrassing the people for whom they work — you, to be exact — but your loyalties are to someone who really doesn't care about good taste or loyalty." I wasn't fired. Nor did things change with our heroine.

Then she decided that she would rather be a travel agent than a secretary. And so it came to happen. I remember that when an error occurred and the client inquired about the mistake, her response was always the same, "Don't concern yourself with it." Towards the end of my time there, I recall one client barking back, "I happen to be a surgeon, and when I don't concern myself, the patient dies." Remarks like these seemed to go over her head, and she ploughed ahead, learning at the expense of the client.

The manager went on holidays for a week, and I noticed that one of the new employees was cheating, in fact stealing from the company. He was very slick, but his manoeuvres were fairly evident to me. I spoke to the owner, telling him how I thought it was being done. I also said that if I had misjudged the gentleman, I would of course apologize. The owner installed himself in our office, watching the day-to-day operation. At the end of the week, the employee was gone. The owner approached me, thanked me for my efforts on his behalf, and promised to put me on profit sharing. It never happened.

VOYAGES BEL-AIR

I stayed eight years with the company, and when I was offered the opportunity to open my own agency, I was ready. I opened Voyages Bel-Air in the Beaconsfield Shopping Centre in 1968. Two friends were helping me decorate the office a few days before the official opening — one was making drapes, the other was ironing. The door opened, and Father Frank McMahon stuck his head in the door and said, "If I decided to go to Ireland this Saturday, would I be your first client?" Well, he *was* our first client, followed very quickly by a host of other friends, relatives and people who had heard about my new office. Nepotism ran rampart, as I hired our sons for office cleaning, and daughter for filing. Gordie kept the home fires burning on Saturdays, when I had to be on hand in the office.

I believe I was one of the first West Island offices to require new employees to be bilingual. Even though I, myself, was not completely fluent in French, I felt it important that clients be served in the language of their choice. I may have excluded some very valuable travel agents, although in 1968, experienced people were few and far between. Training was a haphazard on-the-job thing, and much depended on the validity of the knowledge being dispensed by the trainer, usually the owner. In most cases, he or she lacked proper training because it wasn't available in those days. In my opinion, however, if a very knowledgeable person either owning or managing an agency can train his or her personnel, it can be as valuable as a one-year course. In my case, I had ten years' airline experience, but learned the rest on my own. The agency I first joined had nothing to offer me in training, either in the airline or steamship field. In my present job I was able to learn more about steamship travel, as I had been clueless in this area.

At that time, cruising was not as popular as it now is. Sailing from New York, the sea could be rough until reaching Cape Hatteras, thus eliminating several days of luxury living for those who were confined to their cabins with seasickness. Later came the sailings from

Florida, which made it possible for those without "sea legs" to enjoy the entire voyage. We sold cruises as "Floating Hotels," stressing the "all-inclusive" features and comparing the cost favorably with hotel vacations, considering that transportation by luxury vessel was included in the cost.

I remember that during the time spent in my first travel agency job, Swedish American Line offered me a trip to Quebec City to visit one of their ships, in order to familiarize myself with it. The travel agency told me that if I could sell one of these cruises they would let me go to see the ship. As it turned out, I was determined to have the opportunity to visit this cruise ship, and was successful in selling a cruise on *The Gripsholm*. I was permitted to go to Quebec, where the ship was anchored. As far as I was concerned, this was training in reverse, an exercise in futility, serving only to antagonize an employee. This increased my resolve to be in a position to offer better employee educational opportunities, but I held my counsel and my tongue.

Two ladies booked a cruise out of New York with me. After all arrangements had been made, they informed me that they had a very rare type of monkey, miniature in size, very delicate, frail in fact, and most precious to them. It was important that they bring the monkey with them. I told them that the monkey would have to be kept crated in the baggage department, which offended them somewhat. I said I would call the line in New York, asking if an exception could be made, due to my clients' attachment to the monkey. The answer was "Under no circumstances." I made the unfortunate suggestion that they get a "monkey sitter" and leave their treasure at home. "Would you leave your *child* at home, and go off and enjoy yourself?" My automatic mental reflex was, Try me. I said, instead, "Of course you will be able to visit your monkey in the baggage compartment." "That's not good enough. He must stay in the cabin when we are there, eat with us, and accompany us on all sightseeing tours when we are on land." I cancelled all arrangements, and applied the refund to a Caribbean vacation. I told them if they were planning any trips for their monkey now or in the future, they were specifically not to let me in on the news. They subsequently made all their travel arrangements with me, and not once did we say the word "monkey." I don't know how long that critter lived, but I have the feeling that he was a world traveller before he left this planet for his monkey heaven in the sky.

MRS. X

In the 'sixties, I booked a yearly cruise for a lady and her son. Actually, they liked back-to-back cruises to Bermuda, a total of two weeks. When the ship returned to New York, at the end of one cruise, they would stay on board and do the exact same trip again. This client had difficulty walking, and so staying on board was of added value to her. She would always make the appointment to see me and would bring along her son, who was in his forties. I learned never to look at the son, for she would become angry if I addressed any conversation to him. He was of average height, broad shouldered, somewhat stooped for a man of his age, but was obviously quite strong.

As cruises were quoted in US funds, my client always paid in actual dollars. In order to be of additional service to her, due to her infirmity, I would offer to collect the money from her the day before the funds were required in my office. She always had a little tea-party ready for me, for I think she was lonely. When she produced the US dollars, the odor of mothballs was so overwhelming, I felt nauseous, but managed to hide my discomfort. Every year I dreaded this trip, but each year she asked if I would be coming by, indicating that the ritual was becoming more important to her. In the 1980s Mrs. X stopped travelling. I called her twice a year, and we had a nice conversation, but she said her travelling days were over, as walking was too difficult a problem.

One day, I was told that Mrs. X was in my office – alone. I came out to the main office, took her by the arm, assisted her to my office, and helped her take a seat. In spite of the fact that her hair was disheveled, her face lined with deep wrinkles and there were thick ridges under her clouded blue eyes, she was trying to maintain the dignity that had always been her trademark. Not a word was spoken, and so I remained quiet, holding her hand. I then took my seat behind the desk, my eyes inquiring, and my voice saying, "I'm right here, Mrs. X." Her eyes met mine, and the tears came one by one, dripping down on her mink coat. The silence cut through the room, and still not a word was said. When Mrs. X did begin to speak, her words were almost unintelligible. I strained to catch a word here and there, and through it all the name of her son came to me over and over again. He had thrown her on the bed and twisted her legs around, causing extreme pain. The reason was because she had insisted that he see the family doctor. I didn't know how to help, but asked her if I could call the doctor, whom I knew.

As I awaited a return call from the doctor, I sat holding her hand. My only thoughts were, Imagine being so alone, that the only person you can turn to is someone like me, a stranger, someone who doesn't know what to do. When the call came, I asked the doctor if it was safe for Mrs. X to go home. He said, "Absolutely not." I asked for suggestions from him, but he was helpless and hopeless. I called the police station to find out if there were such things as "safe houses." There were. I called them and they were all full.

I was expected in Montreal, so I asked Mrs. X if she would like to go downtown with me and wait while I attended a very short meeting on Mountain Street. Her eyes met mine, and I saw a momentary glow of hope, which faded in a split second. Bringing the car around to the front door, I was able to get Mrs. X into the front seat without too much difficulty. Her attitude changed. She seemed to be coming back from a long journey, taking in her surroundings as though she recognized them from another time. She began to talk, and I could understand every word.

When we reached Mountain Street, I pulled around to the Ritz Hotel, leaving the car with the doorman. I ushered Mrs. X into the Ritz, directing her to the bar just to the right of the front door. I said I would order tea for her, and would join her soon for a cup and some little cucumber sandwiches that I knew she would enjoy. On the way out, I put a bill into the hands of the manager, asking him to make sure that Mrs. X had very special treatment.

After the meeting, I zipped around the corner and into the Ritz bar. I joined my client, and asked how she was doing. She seemed to have perked up, and was obviously enjoying herself. When the waiter came later with the bill, she looked up at him and asked, "Were you here in 1931?" He replied, "Yes, Madame, I was." "Did you know my husband, Mr. X ?" "Yes, Madame. Mumm's Cordon Rouge." Mrs. X lit up like a Christmas candle. "He died shortly after that," she said. She went into a silent reverie for a few moments, and when she joined me again, her face seemed to have lost all its wrinkles, and the deep circles were not visible. Perhaps the lighting in the Ritz enhanced the worn faces of all its patrons.

My problem was not solved however, as I still did not know where Mrs. X would sleep that night. My sister Phyllis was visiting, and my niece and her husband were due the next day. I would have to pick up my sister at Dorval Airport on the way home from the Ritz.

A little explanation is required here. My sister Phyllis, the nun, had done a great deal of travelling. She was in Uganda in the last horrible days of Idi Amin. She was held at gunpoint on a train in France while the gunman robbed her of the small amount of money she had placed in top of her purse. The *gendarmes* searched every railway car for him. He wasn't aware, however, of the mad money she had stored in a safe place. In short, Sister Phyllis was not a shrinking violet and I knew I could count on her to carry on a conversation with Mrs. X while I kept my eyes on the road.

In all their travels, my sister stayed in what the nuns call "Our House" (a convent run by their order of nuns) in many cities. Bearing this in mind, I will recount some of the conversation between Mrs. X and my sister.

Mrs. X: "And where have you just arrived from, Phyllis?"
Phyllis: "I've just come from our house in Vancouver. I have been away for some time. I'll be staying in our house here for a few days only, after I visit with my sister at her home, then on to another sister in Toronto.
Mrs. X.: It must be nice to have a few houses.
Phyllis: Yes, we have houses in many parts of the world.
Mrs. X: Oh, really, where else do you have houses?
Phyllis: In Canada we have one here, one in Winnipeg and Vancouver. In the Atlantic Provinces we have only one.
Mrs. X: Oh, what a shame! (a roll of the eyes)
Phyllis: Our main house is in Paris
Mrs X: And to think I am looking for a place to stay tonight.

At this juncture I am able to jump in and ask about the weather in Vancouver. During the rapid-fire discourse above, I was racking my brain to see if a bright light would go on and lead me to the solution to my problem. It occurred to me that Mum had a very dear friend who was like an aunt to my siblings and me. On arriving home, after I had seated Mrs. X and my sister, explained to the children, told Gordie that No, I was not running a hospice, I phoned Peggy Coady, our seventy-five- year-old deaf friend. I asked her if she would help me out, and she agreed. Due to her deafness, it was difficult to explain everything without everyone within hearing range knowing about the problem facing Mrs. X. As it turned out, Peggy mistakenly understood that Mrs. X was a nun, who had accompanied my sister to Montreal, and who needed a place to stay. She told me later that she couldn't understand why in God's name a friend of my sister and also a nun, could not have been accommodated in the convent. She said nothing, however, and agreed to host Mrs. X for the night, believing I had a good reason for asking.

That evening I drove Mrs. X to Peggy's. I introduced her to Mrs. X, but being pre-disposed to the idea that she was hosting a nun, and also because of her deafness, Peggy understood me to say "Sister" X rather than "Mrs. X." Being the perfect hostess, she turned the conversation to things that would interest any nun — the Pope's health, what houses "Sister" had visited this summer, and what subjects she taught. Mrs. X seemed to come to life, and joined in the conversation that was taking place in this crazy house. She hadn't had so much fun in a long time. She told of not really liking to stay in houses, but preferred ships. I heard about it the next day from both parties, and wished I had been an invisible guest.

The next morning, Mrs. X didn't need to be entertained, for she spent the morning instructing several brokers on how she wanted her portfolios to be handled. By the afternoon, Mrs. X was back to her old self, requesting that I return her to her son. I went into town to pick her up that evening, and took her back home, where her son welcomed her as though she had been sorely missed. It was sickening to watch this reunion, knowing what I knew. I suppose that in today's world I would have alerted the police of the situation, but then it did not even enter my mind. I stayed for a few minutes, and told both of them that I would be checking on them the next morning. I left them with my home telephone number, but no call came. When I telephoned, I was treated as the travel agent, and no mention was ever made of the sorrow I had witnessed. It never happened. Although I spoke to Mrs. X on the telephone several times, I never saw her again. She joined Mr. X some years ago, and no doubt they are toasting each other at this very moment – with Mumm's Cordon Rouge, of course. I do see the aging son, but he does not recognize me. I wonder.

TRAVEL COURSE

Airline agents drop their work the minute they leave the office. Travel agents tend to have a rapport with their clients, sometimes knowing them socially, and the client will often call the agent at home, to give an additional piece of information or to inquire about a travel point. I remember one Boxing Day as my family and I were spending a relaxing time, looking forward to eating leftover turkey, no cooking today, I received a call from a client who lived in Ottawa. I expected to receive her "Compliments of the Season" greeting, but instead was met with "I'm just planning my annual trip to Portugal in April, and thought I should give you a call right away." I was able to say "Later" in a nice way, but it wasn't easy. Still learning about people.

A similar disturbance occurred one Easter Sunday. My family and I were attending church service and the six of us were heading up the main aisle, carrying the offertory gifts. I heard a loud voice saying, "Mrs. Henchey, how about Ireland?" My mind immediately switched into a travel mode. I turned around and spotting the eager traveller, called out, "Not this year, Fred, Ireland's not ready for you yet." Turning around to join my family, I could see that they were not pleased, but there was nothing I could do or say then. Several faces in the crowd were frowning, and I had the idea that they were thinking, So what's wrong with Ireland? I would have to watch out for my automatic reflexes and practice playing deaf at appropriate times.

Even up until the 1980s, travel agents were getting only on-the-job training, and I always felt that there needed to be some sort of educational program that could be made available by the industry to the public. Nobody seemed to have the time to think about it. That was about to change.

After I had been in the Beaconsfield Shopping Center for fifteen years, Phyllis Blaukopf, the Dean of Adult Education at John Abbott College, approached me. She was setting up fall courses, and was interested in offering a non-credit Travel Course. I was one of only a handful of Certified Travel Consultants in Montreal, was on the Education Committee of the Alliance of Canadian Travel Agents (ACTA), and had had about thirty years of experience in the industry. Having helped the government to write the law (Bill 19) governing Quebec Travel Agents, my qualifications justified her confidence in me. She had also used our travel service, and had obviously been satisfied.

I designed a course for those people who wished to start a second career, or change the direction of an established one. It was for mature students. At the outset, I explained that if the person wished to join the travel industry to make a fortune, perhaps the college could recommend a different course. On the first evening, thirty-five students showed up, most of them surprised that a travel agent's job required hard work, a fair amount of common sense and a lot of study. A generous portion of the course was devoted to airfares, and how to make them work for the customer, getting the best buy for his expenditure. The rest was divided into how and when to use a tour operator, differences in hotels, car rentals, cruises, steamship bookings, insurance, and other ancillary services. For those who passed the exam I gave, and who were interested, I offered placement in a travel agency for training purposes.

The twice-a-year course was very successful, and I later hired instructors who were travel agents and airline people I knew, although I still wrote and directed the course. I found that teachers and nurses were often the class leaders and had good memories for details. They also took excellent notes, and were serious in their intention to establish a different career.

Some of the graduates of the course came to work for us and for other friends in the industry, and many of them are still in the travel field. I used to tell the graduates that what they had learned would give them the confidence they would need to apply for a job, and would be a valuable introduction to all of the tools they would learn to use in the intricate world of travel. At the beginning of the course, I would ask the students why they wanted to join the travel industry. Ninety-nine percent of the time the answer would be, "Because I like to travel." I assured them that in future if they should be on a job interview, this would not impress the prospective boss, for he or she would surely want them to be in his office, working, not globe-trotting. I impressed upon them however, that any good boss would want them to partake in as much training as possible in the office, but also at destinations that were popular with their clients.

TRAVELLING LIGHT

When speaking of training, I am reminded that while I was operating my classes at John Abbott, the president of the national body of ACTA (Alliance of Canadian Travel Agents) asked if I would give a course on cruises to staff members of participating members. They were targeting the younger consultants who had no cruise experience. Now that the cruise industry was becoming a hot travel item, this training was necessary. The course was to take place aboard the Holland American ship, *Volendam,* as it sailed on a week's cruise from New York to Hamilton Harbour, Bermuda, stayed one day, then returned. I had some reluctance about the idea, not because I didn't believe in it, but because I wasn't keen to be away from my family for a week. I did accept the volunteer assignment, however, and I was to regret it.

The cost to any participating agency was $350, a paltry sum for such a valuable experience, and so there was a waiting list for the course. ACTA accepted thirty-five students, a fairly large number, the same as in my John Abbott classes, so I expected the course to go as smoothly as they always went here at home.

On board the ship, the first morning of the course arrived, and I was prepared, having worked for several weeks putting together something that I thought was apropos for young consultants. At nine a.m., standing on the stage of the *Volendam* theatre, I was surprised to see that nobody was in the audience. I waited for some time, until one-by-one or two-by-two, the weary bodies straggled into the theatre. Some dropped their heads down for a little snooze, others put their feet up on the seat in front of them, closed their eyes, and also caught a little shut-eye. I was able to bring the class to order, and explained to them just why they were there. It seemed that some of these people were due a vacation, or overtime, and the agency owner had sent them on a little familiarization trip. Some of them had purchased the trip themselves, and had no intention of being educated on their own dollar. It was the most frustrating thing I had ever done in my life. Most of the students kept the bar and the orchestra going all night, some getting no sleep and coming right to the course, some napping for an hour or so before appearing in the theatre. Some appeared only at lunchtime, still looking haggard and hung-over. I was lucky to have some serious consultants who really wanted to learn, and that was somewhat comforting. There were also agency owners aboard, people who were well versed in the cruise business, who simply wanted an inexpensive cruise, and had no intention of attending the lectures.

Each evening at dinner, I joined a different group at their table, as had been requested by ACTA. I always ordered a fairly good bottle of wine, and tried to be pleasant, getting to know what made these people tick. When I ordered wine at one table, a big buxom woman in her twenties told me, "We don't drink that kind of wine at this table. I always order Dom Perignon." I replied, "Well, please don't let me interrupt your routine." I couldn't believe that such bad manners existed, and wondered how I could instill a few "do's" and "don'ts" into the course. After giving it some thought, I decided that I should do only the job I was asked to do. I couldn't teach these people about courtesy and class in one week. In the final analysis, they didn't want to learn about anything not already in their vocabulary.

Anyone who has been on a cruise will know that there is a lot of pomp and circumstance surrounding the dinner hour, especially when the captain has gone to the trouble of acknowledging a travel group on board. About seventy percent of cruise business is provided by the travel agency industry. I don't know about the prevailing statistics, but I imagine the figure is still quite high. Airlines no longer pay travel agents a fair share of the ticket price – in most cases they now pay nothing. Travel agents have had to develop business in other areas, and all-inclusive cruises have been the beneficiary. Most cruise lines like to acknowledge the business received from travel agents, and do so whenever a group of agents, or a group sponsored by agents, is aboard.

Holland America acknowledged our group, and consequently the captain invited me to sit at his table for dinner one evening, arranging for our students to be located at tables close by. As the captain was entertaining his guests, recounting a tale which had obviously been told many times in similar situations, I happened to take my eyes off of him for a split second, looking over at my charges. There they were, throwing spitballs at each other, from table to table. Those who were not engaging in this indoor sport, were dodging whatever came their way. Some left the dining room in disgust. My mouth hung open until I decided that it might be the wrong place at the wrong time, and I immediately clammed up for security purposes.

The captain came to my rescue. He stood up, saying, "Why don't we have our dessert brought to the lounge, where we can relax and have a good coffee and liqueur." He never referred to the incident, and I didn't apologize for my group. Our eyes had met during the spitball playoffs, and he immediately sensed my mortification and embarrassment. Had he recalled a long ago time when he, himself, had acted with youthful inappropriateness? Did he wish he could have shed his responsibility for a moment or two and joined our reprobates in a good spitball fight? With his regal bearing and a rather stern manner, I couldn't, however, miss the twinkle in his eye that seemed to say, "Been there, done that. Forgiven." He helped me to understand these young people who were just "having a good time." They would learn later the meaning of the word "appropriate." I hoped.

One afternoon after one of the training sessions, a young consultant from Eaton's Travel in Halifax approached me to ask if we could get together for a cup of coffee. After we were seated in the lounge, she apologized for the behaviour of some of her colleagues. She said she could imagine how insulting it was to be treated as I was being treated. I told her that I was used to being given respect, and that while I didn't hold myself responsible for the actions of some of the people on the course, I felt inadequate inasmuch as I was not commanding their respect. She asked me if I would repeat after her, "I don't give a shit." I said I couldn't do that, for the word was not in my vocabulary. After pleading that I should do it for my own sake, and if not, at least for hers, I relented and said, "I don't give a shit." She then asked me to say "I *don't* give a shit," and then "I don't *give* a shit, and so on. I was really getting the hang of this. She insisted that I say each sentence with great feeling, and as I did so it began to feel very good. At the end of the session, I really "*didn't* give a shit." The next day, I marched into the theatre, mounted the stage, and said, "Anyone who wishes to leave, please do so now, or sit up straight and do what you were sent here to do: *learn*." To my surprise, no one left, and they all opened their eyes, straightening up in their seats. What a victory! Thank you, Miss Halifax. If only I could remember your name.

After the last session, my job was done. I could relax and enjoy what remained of the journey. On arrival back in New York, we discovered that the dockworkers were on strike, and there would be no assistance with our baggage. Some of my students approached me on the dock, asking if I would be responsible for taking their luggage to the taxi area. They were boarding different flights to their hometowns. By this time, I was well armed to answer their request with a, "No, this is something you'll have to do yourselves." I was travelling light, due to many years of experience boarding flights, but my own baggage was all I could manage. I wanted to be on my own, free again. I gave them directions, however, and waited until all of them were on their way before I headed to the airline terminal and a pay phone, where I could call home.

While the best part of going away is to return to the sanctuary of our homes, I had never before had the yearning I experienced at the time of dialing the Montreal area code, and our number. At long last, on the third ring Betty Anne picked it up. Almost in tears of joy, I said, "Hi, how are you, dear?" A silence. "Betty Anne?" And then a river of tears poured over the phone line. "What is it, my dear little girl?" (She was about twenty.) "Kevin and I broke up again." I wanted to say, Betty Ann, can you say "I don't give a shit?" but I was back in my "mother" role. I was needed again. I was home. I had returned to my pedestal, and how comfortable that felt. We agreed that we would have a cup of tea and talk as soon as I was back where I belonged. In the years that followed, I had many occasions when that expression flooded my mind, but up to now I have kept it in storage there. Just thinking it, however, has sometimes saved the day.

THE GREEN LADY

From the cruise episode, it would seem that my opinion of those people who work in the travel industry is indeed very low. On the contrary, I have a great deal of respect for mainstream travel agents. For the most part, they are industrious, honest, knowledgeable, well travelled, and an excellent source of information. Their livelihood depends on suppliers whom they endeavour to represent fairly. After consultation with the client, they make recommendations, but always leave the ultimate decision in the hands of the buyer. Their incomes are lower than those in other businesses, reduced-rate travel and an interesting environment compensating in some measure. Their comparative shopping services are used even more today by those who have no intention of booking with them, but merely want to make sure that their dot-com rates are the best they can find. This includes hotels, cruises, car rentals, and airfares. Bargains are always available, but what the bargains generally lack is any form of customer service. In customer service, the travel agencies outdo most businesses by a country mile. It is what their business is all about. Their *service* is what separates the bargains from the good buys, the pig-in-a-poke vacation from the heavenly holiday.

Over the years, I have worked with many travel consultants, and have had a good relationship with those competitors who were striving to upgrade the level of travel agents in general. During discussions, the one thing that always caught my attention was their devotion to the client, and a willingness to go the extra mile in research to ascertain that they were providing the best advice available. So here's to them, as they struggle to keep open their offices, in spite of difficulties being imposed by the airlines that ignore the fact that travel agents have been building the airline business for over sixty years.

When I opened my office, I had one hard and fast rule. If a consultant made a mistake, it was important that I be told immediately, so that together we could fix it. I could tolerate a lot of things, but I said I would not tolerate any employee lying to me, perhaps blaming an airline, a tour company or even the client for something that was clearly our fault. I thought this arrangement was working rather well. I had just hired a new employee, and she had been with us for about a week. Very nervously, she asked if she could have a few minutes of my time. I invited her into my office, and pointed to a chair, for by the look of her, I feared she would faint at any moment. Her first words were, "I lied to you," haltingly, in a whisper. I said, "Well, fifty percent of your problem is over, now that you have told me. Have you made a mistake, and don't know how to fix it?" "No," she replied. "I told you I was twenty-one, but I'm only eighteen."

We ironed out the problem, and this young lady, Martine Coté, became a very good travel consultant. She later left to become a Sales Representative for Sabena, the Belgian Airline. A few years after that she went into partnership with a colleague, and opened a tour company, selling it last year for several million dollars. Was it the honesty that paid off? I telephoned her to offer her my congratulations. She seemed very surprised that after so many years I would still be proud of her accomplishments. I still am.

A very weird situation occurred in the mid-'seventies, just before all international flights were transferred from Dorval to Mirabel Airport. A fairly new employee had come to my home for dinner, after which I was to give her some training. We had just finished eating when I had a call from the manager of British Airways. He told me that my Russia-bound group was having difficulties, and he needed me to assist them. That was odd, for I had no group leaving that evening. Had that been the case, a staff member or I would have accompanied them to the airport to make sure everything was in order. As it turned out, the group had been booked by our downtown office. The manager of that branch was at the airport and had asked the airline to call me for assistance.

Francine, our new employee, wished to be of some help if possible, and also to experience this facet of our business that she found incompatible with what she thought would be the duties of a travel agent. Off we went. On arrival at the British Airways ticket counter, I was handed a walkie-talkie, and told that the problem was at the departure gate. It seems that passenger after passenger was becoming ill. I headed for the British Airways gate. Assembled there, among other passengers, were forty physical education teachers, accompanied by their group leader who was taking them to Russia to experience the Russian physical education program.

Some seemed fine, others were lying on the floor. Two had been removed from the aircraft and placed on the floor with the others. On closer inspection, I could see that the ones on the floor were in some pain, their eyes rolling in their heads. Having no medical training, I was almost paralyzed with fear. I spoke to British Airways on the walkie-talkie, asking if there were doctors available in the airport and was told there were no doctors assigned to the airport. This was incredible. After so many years in the business, I had not known this, nor given it a thought. What an important oversight on the part of our federal government, is what went through my mind. Ah, but there was a nurse. I asked that they call her.

Miss Roberge arrived, and what a godsend she was. She arranged for blankets and pillows to be delivered. She showed me how to use a tongue depressor in order to make sure that no one swallowed his or her tongue. She called every hospital to see who could take these people, and was turned down by each and every one. I called Stan Knox, the administrator of the Lakeshore General Hospital, but was unable to get through to him at home. As we did these things, we kept a close eye on the passengers. I would look at a person, he would seem fine, and then in a split second, would turn grey and his eyes would roll. I followed all of the instructions given to me by Miss Roberge. We worked as a team, doing our best to help these terrified individuals. British Airways would not allow another member of my staff to enter the departure lounge.

I instructed British Airways to remove all the passengers' luggage from the aircraft. I asked Francine to call all local hotels so see who could put up this number of people for the night. We booked them on the flight the next evening, in case they could travel.

Miss Roberge informed me that she had previously worked for a doctor associated with the Lachine General Hospital. She was able to reach him, to see if he could have our passengers accepted there, for they had previously refused to do so. He performed his magic, and said to bring everyone over. Although there were no beds available, he would meet us in the entrance hall, and handle us there.

I chartered a bus, and shepherded our group onto it. Those who were very sick rallied enough to walk on to the bus. Those who had not yet been ill were very frightened that they would be next. I walked up and down the darkened bus, touching each head saying, "You're safe. I'm here with you." A young California woman travelling with her friend, grabbed onto my leg, and said, "Don't leave us, green lady." I was wearing a green pantsuit.

On arrival at the hospital, staff members came out to assist our passengers into the lobby. All the passengers sat or lay down on the floor. Several doctors and nurses appeared and began to take temperatures and blood pressures. In deference to my age, I suppose, a chair had been provided for me. When the doctor assigned to my case began to take my blood pressure, I told him that I was not part of the group. He insisted however, and found that I was the only one with elevated blood pressure. "Aha," he said, "just as I suspected." And he left. What did that mean?

Two of our passengers were hospitalized. The doctors pieced together the actions of the passengers in the hours before they checked into the airport. All of them had come on a chartered bus (not arranged by our company) that had stopped at a little motel restaurant on Upper Lachine Road so they could have a bite to eat. Forty of the passengers had eaten the coleslaw. These were the ones ill with ptomaine poisoning. All but two would be able to continue on to Russia the next evening.

While sitting in the lobby, keeping an eye on the passengers, I happened to look down, and was shocked to see that my green suit was covered in blood. I asked Francine to get some towels and other supplies from the nurse, and find out where the ladies' room was located. What a help she was. When she returned, I placed a towel around me, as though I had just stepped out of a sauna, took the supplies, and headed for the ladies room. I removed all my clothes from the waist down, rinsed them in the tiny sink, and rolled them in one of the towels. They were still very wet, but I put them on again and proceeded to the lobby, placed a towel on the chair and reclaimed my seat. It seemed that I hadn't been missed, nor had anyone noticed my strange behaviour. Preoccupied with their situation, the worries of my precious charges transcended any activities around them, usual or unusual. About five o'clock in the morning, a news reporter interviewed me. The pants were starting to dry, but, thank God, he didn't mention them. We appeared on the eleven o'clock news with the usual hoopla reserved for evenings when nothing startling was happening in Montreal or other parts of the world.

Francine and I arrived at my home just after six a.m. I told her to go to bed in the guest room, and not to come to the office in the morning. I slept late, but was in the office at my usual time. I was able to tie up the loose ends with our downtown office regarding the departure on British Airways for those in the group able to travel.

I received a few cards from some of the passengers, one addressed to "The Green Lady." I wish now that I had kept them for I appreciated the fact that even in their confusion, pain and fear they remembered what they had considered a kindness. I considered it a duty, and those sweet people who were far from home needed a friend.

Within a few weeks I had another emergency situation that took place in my office. *I* was the emergency, and found myself being transported to the Lakeshore General Hospital, where I underwent an operation. I suppose I should have presented myself there instead of staying at the Lachine General the evening of our famous British Airways "non-departure," but looking back on it, I think I knew that this group needed a "protector" as well as a friend. I still feel that in hospitals we do need "protectors," for in emergencies, we cannot always speak for ourselves.

BETTY ANNE

In 1974, Gordie was transferred to London, England, for a year. Our three boys were in university, and our daughter was to begin her last year of high school. We decided that I would stay home with the children, we would visit each other regularly throughout the year, and take a family holiday in the summer. Betty Anne asked if she could accompany her father to England, and take her last year in a boarding school. This wasn't such a bad idea, for we knew of such a school — The Sacred Heart Convent, a sister school of the one I had attended in Montreal. In fact, my sister Phyllis had a "house" there! We wired the school in late August, and after several inquiries on their part, received the telegram we awaited. Such excitement when Betty Anne was accepted!

The day came for our departure. On arrival at Dorval Airport, a group of about forty of our daughter's "best friends" were waiting to bid farewell to her. They hugged and kissed, and with each embrace, I could see my daughter becoming less and less sure that she wanted to leave these fine people.

As we checked into the flight, Gordie realized that even though we were loaded with baggage, we had left a carrying case in the hall cupboard. There was no one at home except the dog, Twiggy, and it was because of her that in those days we never locked our doors. We remembered this, and called a cab. Gordie went home, grabbed the case and raced back to the airport, just as the agent was telling us they could wait no longer for the baggage. Saved by our Twiggy and the cab driver.

I accompanied Gordie to England in order to find suitable accommodations for him. We wanted a two-bedroom flat so that Betty Anne could spend weekends in London with him. We arrived on a Sunday, spending the day in the Chesterfield Hotel, where Alcan had permanent accommodations for their travellers. We had afternoon tea in the lounge, as Betty Anne hid her tears, having convinced herself that she had lost all her friends by going to England for a year. "What a mistake I've made," was the tea-time theme.

Each day, after Gordie left for the office, I checked the newspapers for suitable accommodations. I made and kept about six appointments a day. It was a time of high rents in return for low quality.

It rained every single day, and I was becoming quite discouraged. The highlight of the day, however, was tea in the lounge of the Chesterfield. I met Betty Anne there every day after my flat hunting was completed. The tea-time topic was as usual the friends she had abandoned and who would forget her in the space of a year. Each day was a little cheerier, and by the third day, Betty Anne had developed a lifetime loyalty to afternoon tea.

I finally decided to engage the services of a good rental agent and went to his office. I waited for some time for the person at the desk to raise her head and actually be aware that someone was waiting. Backed up by several other rental agents, they too were writing important memos and were too engrossed to sense that a potential client was waiting in the wings. I noted also that telephones were ringing, and I began counting the rings before each was acknowledged. I believe the lowest number was seventeen rings. I was about to leave, when a darling little man stuck his head around a door, saying "Hal–o-o-o, are you waiting to see me?" I was tempted to say that I was waiting to see anyone who could see me, but instead I said, "Yes, I think you are the person who can help me." After explaining to him exactly what I needed, he asked me to wait in the outer office.

After an hour or so, I was becoming restless, and in fact the ringing phones were getting on my nerves. When the gentleman poked his head around the door again, I asked if I at least could help his overworked staff by answering the telephone. He thought that was a splendid idea, and gave me a pad and pen to jot down notes on what the caller was requesting.

I worked all day, except for lunch when the little old gentleman took me next door for a sandwich. It was very easy work, for all of the callers were Canadians re-locating. Being in the same boat, it wasn't difficult to ask pertinent questions. When it came to location, location, location, I was lost, but assured the callers that our manager would sort that out himself when he returned their calls. I wondered why they didn't have a "Requirements" form for their people to fill in, making their job much easier. I was to learn first-hand, and from Gordie, that the business world in England moves at a different pace and in a different fashion from ours.

At the end of the day, my friend had found "just the ticket" for us. Gordie joined us, inspected the property, signed the lease, and everything was "tickety-boo." I heartily endorse the way this gentleman worked. He supplied everything I had asked for, and did it in a very quiet manner, no fanfare. I have yet to figure out what kept the heads of his staff glued to blank paper. I don't know what happened to all those other Canadians whose requests I noted for the boss. I gave him a stack of messages at the end of the day. Although he didn't even glance through them, I had the feeling that each and every one would be called. *When* that would happen is what I could not attest to.

We drove to the boarding school one afternoon to meet the headmistress and other staff members. We were completely charmed by those we encountered, as they described life in their wonderful establishment. School uniforms were chosen, and we were pleased that Betty Anne seemed to be somewhat less worried about the life she had left behind.

School would start the following Monday, and so it was arranged that after I returned to Montreal, Gordie would take Betty Anne to school. She did mention that perhaps she could return home with me and forget all about her request to attend boarding school. The die had been cast, however, and there was no turning back. I remembered the old adage, "Be careful what you ask for." I returned home with no other thought in my mind other than wondering what happened when Gordie took Betty Anne to the school to begin her year.

As it happened, they arrived at the school and Betty Anne's roommate was waiting to show her around. They talked for a little while, then there were gales of laughter, and our daughter suggested that perhaps her father could leave. A smile, a hug and a kiss, and she was gone. A whole new life was beginning. She drank in every moment, enthralled with each new experience. There were girls from many different countries, with different cultures, and being exposed to this variety of lifestyles was a broadening experience. Another broadening experience was the intake of starchy foods prevalent at boarding schools. It was a lucky break that our daughter could stand to put on a few pounds during the time spent in England.

Each weekend, our daughter invited a different young lady to her father's flat. He enjoyed the company of the giggly pair, and it helped to pass the time. We had deposited at the school an amount of spending money for Betty Anne. It was a very limited sum set by the school, about £2 weekly, I believe. On one of the weekends a young Arab girl was a visitor and she and Betty Anne went shopping. On arrival home, my daughter proceeded to unload the first of many shopping bags, all loaded with very expensive clothing. Her friend had as many bags, and as many outfits. On being asked how this had happened, Betty Anne's friend informed Gordie that her family paid no attention to the allowance rule, and furthermore she had her own credit cards. If Betty Anne had wanted a car, her friend would have purchased it for her. Needless to say, Gordie explained the facts of life, and our two heroines were marched back to the department store to return the goods.

After a few months, my daughter had developed a little British accent. She rode the underground like a Londoner, did well in school, and developed many friendships, but always longed for her old friends in Beaconsfield. As the years rolled by, Betty Anne had several positions that required some travel, and of course her favourite spot was London. She had found a second home.

PETER

In 1975, our son Peter joined me in the agency. He had been studying Hotel and Restaurant Administration at Ryerson College in Toronto. His decision to have a career in the travel industry meant that I had a trainee who was ready and willing to learn from me.

Our office was open on Thursday evenings. About six o'clock I was just leaving for home, when a frequent traveller came into the office. She said that she and her husband had decided to take their teenage son and daughter to Jamaica on Saturday, two days hence. It was Easter weekend, and not a seat was available to the Caribbean and hotels had been sold out for months. I was not able to stay in the office, due to a previous commitment, so I handed the booking over to Peter who was on duty that evening. My client seemed nervous that a twenty-one-year-old would be handling her difficult request, but I assured her that if anything could be done, Peter would do it for her. The next day I asked Peter about the booking. He said he had cleared some space, but had had to make some long distance calls, a record of which I could find on the file. I was happy that everything had been settled.

About ten days later, my client walked into the office, ignored Peter, and asked to see me in my office. She said, "Peter lied to me." I was so shocked I couldn't answer. She saw the expression on my face, and hastened to add, "He told me that Round Hill in Jamaica was the 'Playground of Millionaires.' Well, let me tell you otherwise. It was the 'Playground of Billionaires'." She had been as impressed as she had wished to be. Her daughter had danced with Hollywood stars, and her son had met starlets who dazzled him. She and her husband had been in seventh heaven. I asked her why she had not wanted to talk to Peter. She said that such praise should first go to the boss, to make sure that he or she is fully aware of the compliments being heaped on an employee. Peter arrived home that evening with a boxed bottle of the best gin, along with two crystal glasses, a gift from his client. I think he was pleased, although in his usual style, he said very little about it. I noticed, however, that my favourite client seemed to find my services superfluous, and was seen frequently discussing her next trip with Peter, her travel consultant.

Voyages Bel-Air / P. Lawson Travel lost Peter to bigger and better ventures in Toronto. Ten years later, he returned to his beloved Montreal, and opened his own agency that he still operates downtown as Voyages P. Henchey Travel. In good travel market times or bad, Peter has been successful. I always tease him about being so good because of his excellent training. He claims it was the minimum wage I paid him that sent him off to greener pastures. We compromise on "a little of both."

MICHAEL

Our first-born son, Michael, developed a penchant for travel at an early eleven months, when his paternal grandparents began picking him up every Friday and transporting him to the Laurentians, where they had built their retirement home. At about age three, having watched "Papa" inspect the property as soon as they arrived each spring, Michael, with a proprietary air, took on this duty. He was very observant, never missing even the smallest crack or evidence that a mouse had found its way into the basement. Rawdon was his second home, and the reason why he now prefers to live in the Laurentians. They call it nostalgia.

One Friday afternoon, when Michael was about seven years old, his grandfather called to say he was running late. Would we be able to put Michael in the care of the conductor of the Beaconsfield-Montreal train, and he would meet Michael in Montreal West. We were somewhat reluctant, but were assured by the stationmaster that our child would be very well taken care of. But something went wrong, and Michael was deposited in Westmount, not Montreal West. Being a curious child, he made a thorough inspection of the station, getting his bearings. While checking out the train tracks (a spear pierces my heart as I visualize the scene) he spotted a railwayman riding a handcar in the direction from which Michael had just arrived. Seeing an opportunity, he asked the man if he was going as far as Montreal West, and sure enough that is where he was headed. What a shock for his grandfather, when Michael alit from the handcar, entered the station, and asked his grandfather to come outside to meet his new friend. Our son was and is very resourceful.

Discussing this event over forty years later, and in light of the macabre headlines about the kidnapping or attacks on children every day, we ask ourselves why we would have placed Michael on that train. Why did Michael's grandfather not notify the police? A different time, a different set of rules. We didn't hear about terrible things being done to children as parents do today. The only kidnapping I had heard or read about was the Lindbergh baby in the early 'thirties. That was long ago and far away, and we were now living in an age where the streets were safe. I cannot imagine any of my grandchildren being left alone for even one minute. Not on a train, not anywhere. Do we feel guilt? No, for that's the way it was.

COMETH THE ICE-CREAM MAN

Before Michael entered the University of Montreal, he wanted to spend a year at the University of Grenoble in France. Presto! He would finance the trip by opening his own summer business. He would be the ice cream man.

This required an initial investment from the parent bank, to be paid back at the earliest possible moment. It was necessary to purchase a three-wheel bike, to which a cooler was attached. Gordie had been in the insulation business, and he assisted Michael in building a very fine cooler to hold the precious popsicles to be sold in our town at the swimming pool. At the close of a week, everything was in place and Michael was in business.

Each day, I would drive him into the Elmhurst Dairy (now Sealtest) in Montreal West, to pick up his order. The popsicles and other delights were packed in dry ice, and were transferred to our freezer until Michael was ready to go on his route. At that time, he loaded the cooler and set off, his body bowed with the weight of the bike and cooler. His goods were sold out in record order, and he would return home to reload several times, returning to the pool at peak periods for highest returns. When his bicycle was parked in the driveway, little children would ring our doorbell and ask for "The Ice-cream Man," clutching their nickels and dimes in their tiny fingers. When the bicycle was not in the driveway, they came anyway, and I would sometimes give them treats if they would sing a song for us. Even the shyest of the bunch would step forward to warble a note or two, not to be deprived of any surprises being handed out.

After three years of this enterprising endeavour, Michael had saved enough to transport himself to Grenoble to study for a year. We would miss him terribly, but at the same time admired his work ethic, and his stick-to-it-iveness. But what of his work? Onto the stage stepped our son Brian, eager to fill Michael's shoes in the ice-cream business.

During the previous year, the city of Beaconsfield had enacted a law stating that no vendors would be permitted in our town without a city licence. Brian dutifully applied for this but was denied on the grounds that selling food was unsanitary. We disagreed with this ruling, as the food came packed in dry ice, and stayed that way during the few hours it was in the cooler. We advised our son to test the law.

It was with fear and trepidation that Brian, laden with his goodies, pedalled to the Beaconsfield pool. Halfway through the afternoon, a police car parked close to the pool, and two burly officers approached the ice-cream bicycle. A ruined career, and then to jail, said our salesman to himself as he watched the approach of two uniformed constables, their scowls visible as they prepared to make their arrest. "Do you have a license to sell this stuff?" asked the first. "No, Sir," replied Brian. There was a pause, as the officers thought about their next step. Second officer: "Do you know it is against the law to do what you are doing?" "Yes, sir," said Brian. Both officers retreated for consultation. Some time passed. The first officer returned saying, "I'll have lemon." The second burly guy in the police car called, "Bring me grape." And so the second Ice Cream Man was able to continue his career for a few summers. He graduated later to building pools and hauling furs for the Hudson Bay Company, but when reminiscing, always has stories to tell about the little kids he met on his ice-cream route, and those who called on him at home, hoping to catch him after-hours with a popsicle looking for an owner.

Later, after one summer job on the railway in British Columbia, Michael decided to visit Hawaii. After several days, he found that even with the trade winds, the island was a little too warm for his taste, and the commercialism offended his sensibilities, so he headed for Alaska. There he found the weather ideal, the landscapes breathtaking and the people warm, friendly and unpretentious. Well worth a return visit.

After his year in Grenoble, Michael cycled along the Riviera, and upon viewing the opulence on display at every turn, knew that this area would not welcome the likes of him on his bicycle. He switched his itinerary to one more accommodating to his tastes, winding up his trip in Paris, having accomplished all he had set out to do, without ever asking for or accepting help from us. Armed with his degrees from the University of Montreal and McGill University, Michael eventually opened his own business, and has been successful in the computer analysis field.

BRIAN

Our son Brian accompanied us on visits to Florida, Bahamas, Barbados, and of course made frequent trips to the Laurentians. His heavy soccer schedule as a player for many Beaconsfield representative teams took him across the city frequently for many tournaments. Travel on a small scale! I remember once when he was playing in Verdun, we happened to sit in the wrong section, so were surrounded by parents of the players on the opposing team. It was a very important game. Brian, a big fellow, was the captain of the Beaconsfield team and wearing Number 8 as usual. The fans were shrieking and yelling at the players. One "lady" started to yell, "Get that Number 8. Kill that Number 8." Others took up the chant. I was absolutely shocked, turning around, and in a small voice said, "Not my little boy...." Everyone laughed, the shouting stopped on a dime, and I could resume breathing.

On another occasion, sitting in the proper stand in Beaconsfield, I was becoming quite upset because Brian's coach was cursing and swearing at his players. His fifteen-year-olds were all very dedicated, and yet he always swore at them, which I thought was unacceptable. Never having missed any of the games, it was becoming more and more obvious to me that each "pep talk" was not just "a slip of the tongue." At half time, I said to the woman who was sitting beside me, "I'm just going to have a word with the coach." When I was able to speak to him, I told him that while Brian was on Mr. F.'s team, we felt that Mr. F. was representing the parents of all the boys. Our son certainly was not accustomed to that kind of language at home. I said that if it didn't stop, we would remove Brian from his team. He was very polite, but said very little. When I returned to the stands, my neighbour asked me what I had said to the coach. When I told her, she said, "Good for you. I've been telling him that for years. He's my husband."

Brian's first trip overseas was when he played for Quebec in Holland. I believe the budget was very tight, for the players ate airline food the whole time they were there. Brian didn't talk much about that trip so I know they didn't win. Without a win, there was never much conversation.

With his own three children actively engaged in soccer and hockey, Brian is again on the travel circuit. He coaches hockey, lacrosse and soccer and is the oldest player on his own soccer team. Apart from a little knee problem, he manages well on the soccer field, for a man about to turn forty-eight.

Having been transferred several times to different parts of Canada, I think Brian always made it a point to check the soccer situation before he accepted the transfer. That's just a little joke we have between us. Fortunately Brian's wife, Lisa, is also a sports enthusiast. Her father, Ken Lane, is an Olympic silver medallist, having carried the flag for Canada in 1952. In May 2003, he was inducted into the Olympic Hall of Fame. So the Henchey children are all sports oriented, which keeps them busy and out of trouble, and they have heroes who inspire them.

We were devastated when, while playing for Loyola, Brian was hit in the first three minutes of the game. He was taken to the Queen Elizabeth Hospital, where he lay for five days in severe pain. The doctor thought he had cracked ribs, uncertain as to whether or not there was something else amiss.

Due to an error, Brian was released, and while wheeling him out of the hospital, Gordie met the doctor, who asked where he thought Gordie was going with our son. He then returned Brian to his room, examined him again, and rushed Brian to the operating room, where his spleen was removed. He then contracted hepatitis, probably due to the many transfusions that he received. He was sixteen and looked like an old man. Later we were told that had Brian been en route to our home when his spleen had ruptured, his life would have been in jeopardy. How blessed we were.

Later, after his recovery, my sister Rita asked Brian if he would return to soccer. He replied that he certainly would, but from now on would give one warning to those intent on getting his number. He has operated that way in sports ever since.

After Brian graduated from Western University, he decided to take some extra courses. He chose Calgary, for they had the best team. On returning to Toronto to look for a job, he was told by a friend that CIBC was looking for a model to represent the modern-day, clean-cut graduate in whom they were interested. The modelling job paid $50, and Brian was chosen for the shoot. The picture appeared on the cover of the CIBC prospectus that year. While in their offices, Brian filled in an application form. Voila! He joined the CIBC team on their Management Course and became a banker by trade.

THE BIKER

In our retirement, Florida was a favourite getaway spot. One year when my sister Rita and I were in Pompano Beach, it was cold and windy, and we had to look for indoor entertainment to while away the evenings. Our usual bridge games were not an option any more, due to the rapid deterioration of Rita's eyesight, brought on by macular degeneration. Videos were the best choice because I could pause and explain to her what was happening in the story when there was no dialogue.

Each evening Rita and I presented ourselves at the local video store, in order to make our choices. The first evening, we were served by a young man who was obviously the owner, judging by the high quality of his service. This young man treated us as royalty, asking all kinds of questions to determine exactly what kind of movies we liked. It all boiled down to a few requirements: Must be a great story, very little violence, although we didn't mind murder if was done in a sophisticated way, no bad language, and we would take any movies starring Clint Eastwood or Jack Lemmon, no matter what the content. After about fifteen minutes our man had chosen two movies, and although I don't recall the titles, I do know that we were very pleased.

We returned the next night and the next. Each time, our video man had prepared a list of three to five movies for our selection. We never had to wait, and he was always on the money as far as the choice was concerned. I think he had labelled us "Little old ladies — not too bright — needing guidance." He became like an adopted son. We began to relish our visits to his store, wondering what surprises he had prepared for us. This continued for three weeks, until one sad day when he was no longer there, no word from him, no selections. In his place, confronting us, was a burly wind-burned young man, with a very thick neck and arms to match. He had slicked-down, jet black hair, resembling a newly tarred road. His eyes were unfriendly, black as coal, never looking head-on, but shifting from side to side, like little peas on a roll, searching for a resting place. He was covered in black leather from neck to toe, and the shirt opened to the waist revealed several gold chains. His chest was a forest of glistening black curls, and I wondered if they were real, or had he velcroed a woolen mat to himself. But it was not a question that I would dwell on for long, as Biker Boy was impatient to get any business out of the way so he could make a call on the cellphone he held in his hand.

We did inquire about the person who had been there previously. He told us that he was his brother. What a shock! Our confidence was somewhat restored however, knowing he was related to our wonder boy. Misplaced confidence. He treated us like morons, little old ladies who had not only lost their looks but their minds as well. He was rude, and we were both afraid of him. I chose the movies, having had the experience of watching our salesman for the previous three weeks. No words were spoken, no "Thanks" or "Come Again." Just pay the money and get out as quickly as possible.

Our last night arrived, and we knew which movies we wanted. We did our business quickly, and I told him this would be our last night. Did I think this would soften his heart? Why in the world would I share this news with him? Of course, I received no reply. I then said (will I ever learn?), "Is that your Harley outside?" A smirk of a smile and, "Yes, Ma'am, that there's my baby. I polish her up good every day, and she performs miracles for ole Dad Boy. Now that's a lady." I knew then that we would never cut it in his perception of class. As we approached the door, Biker Boy called out to us, "Would you two young ladies care for a ride on my Harley?"

What's this? We can join the club? I narrowly missed walking into the glass door. My sister's shock was well hidden when she declined demurely, but never having been on a motorcycle, this little old lady accepted with pleasure. Biker Boy mounted the machine and I climbed on behind him, donning the helmet that had been on his greasy mop only hours before. As I did so, every joint in my body screamed at me, Are you out of your mind? I knew I was, but this was a thrill I had never experienced, so, "Damn the torpedoes." There was a gentleman in there somewhere, for he did go helmetless on my account.

No sooner had the motorcycle started to move, than I became terrified. Biker Boy had hated us from the start — probably hates all women. I am not safe here. My life is at risk, and not from the Harley. We were flying along, and my eyes were riveted on the hair in front of me — not one strand was out of place. I believed that he relished the freedom of being helmetless, and this was an excuse to appear gentlemanly. His hair was a showcase of his control, a control that he would exercise over me in time. My philosophizing lead me into a state of panic. My head began to pound and my heart was jumping to and fro saying, Save me, save me. The Harley, true to form, travelled almost as fast as my heart and when Biker Boy hollered, "Hold me tighter," I envisioned the tabloid headlines reading, "Seventy-year old Canadian tourist murdered by twenty-five-year-old biker lover," and later in the story, "Black curly hairs were found under the woman's fingernails, indicating a struggle. Later forensic science indicated that these were not human hairs, but synthetic, the type found in popular welcome mats."

The ride became wilder and wilder, until suddenly Mr. Biker pulled into a shopping center and drove around to the back. He stopped on a dime, nearly catapulting me over his head and into the nearest dumpster. Dumpster! my mind cried, and it all became clear. He hated women so much, he would put me in the dumpster, rape and murder me. Nobody knew who we were so the crime would never be solved. He had probably murdered our adopted son, who no doubt was lying cold and dead in the back of the video store. How could we have believed he was the brother of our video man? Gullible, that's what we were.

Biker Boy disembarked from the Harley, and I knew my number was up. I said in a very weak voice, "So this is where it ends?" "Yes m'am. You see that dumpster behind the arts and crafts store? I check it out almost every day. Oh, Man, do I get some beauties out of there!" Oh, Dear God, he has an accomplice who leaves *his* handiwork in the dumpster for inspection. Oh, God, I don't want to die — especially tonight — we have Clint Eastwood. "I have enough pearls and sprinkles to make my partner a beaded choker. I'll start it right after I finish the pearl studded sweater I'm knitting for him. I was going to check out that goldmine of a dumpster now, but your sister will be waiting for you. Next stop, video store!"

Life took on a whole new meaning. I was spared for another day. As for my sister, she never expected to see me again. She knew the biker would kill me and if he didn't, *she* would, for she had spent the time outside the store, blind, unable to see any oncoming threat. She spent those moments in fear of her own life, a drive-by shooting, perhaps a mugging? Her main thoughts, however, were for me who had most assuredly gone to meet my Maker. As my friend and I pulled up outside the store, Rita let out an awful cry that she had been stifling. We kissed and hugged, both glad to be still among the land of the living.

That evening we watched Clint, and when he uttered his famous words, "Go on, make my day," my thoughts drifted back to my day, one part of me saying, That was a really stupid move, and another saying. Go on, make my day.

As for Biker Boy, can such an artsy crafty guy be all bad?

VOYAGES BEL-AIR / P. LAWSON TRAVEL

My travel agency became a part of the larger group owned by P. Lawson Travel, with a hundred offices across Canada. Carlson Marketing group of Minneapolis, Minnesota, had an interest in the company, and later owned it outright. Today the company is known as Carlson Wagon-Lit. The American influence changed things somewhat. They never seemed to understand that in Canada, and especially in Quebec, we do things differently. Our advertising is gentler, wooing rather than pushing the consumer. Differences were ironed out, and we continued to be a well-respected agency.

Every year the managers competed for the ACTA president's highest award, a beautiful diamond ring. It was presented at the yearly management meeting, held in various parts of the world. My office won that award, and I am looking at the diamond ring as I write. It was a great achievement, and how proud I was of the wonderful staff, to my mind, the best in the business.

My life in the travel business changed dramatically in 1983 when I was promoted to Vice-President of Voyages Bel-Air/P. Lawson Travel, responsible for the province of Quebec and the Atlantic Provinces. I could no longer work in Beaconsfield. My office would be in Place Ville Marie, in Montreal, which meant longer travel hours, unfamiliar surroundings, and travel almost daily from there to visit the thirteen offices which would come under my jurisdiction. There would be very little contact with actual passengers; I would be devoting my time to the trials and tribulations of our managers and their profit centres. I would be negotiating with airlines, tour operators and other providers of service in order to insure the best possible services and price structures for our large volume of business.

While it was a very challenging position, and I enjoyed the opportunity of venturing into new territory, I never lost the nostalgia I always felt when I entered my old office in the Beaconsfield Shopping Centre. I wanted to again be a part of that group of people who gave so much of themselves to each other, and to our clients. It was a safe place, one that I knew and loved. I could never again be a part of that family, as it was important to maintain a distance because of possible situations that might occur in the future. None of those imagined situations ever came about, but nonetheless I maintained a somewhat detached attitude. On looking back, I don't regret accepting the position, but it never provided the happy times I had had when I was working with a group of travel agents and clients. I would have preferred to go back to working directly with them, but I learned in fact that the expression, "You can never go back," was indeed true.

After several years in this position I decided that I would like to spend more time at home, perhaps doing voluntary fund raising for worthwhile causes. I telephoned John Powell, the president, in Toronto and discussed this with him, saying I would stay as long as it took to get a replacement. He asked me to give him one more year, and I agreed. During that year, I was restless to start a new life, perhaps working part-time and volunteering a few hours a week. I found the drive to and from work more tiresome, and I knew I had made the right decision to move on. The year was a busy one, and that helped to get me over this particular period.

In February of 1989, I wrote out my resignation, leaving it in a drawer for a week, so that I would be sure I really wanted to leave. At the end of the week, I handed it to my secretary for processing, having given enough thought to the decision. I signed the letter. The deed was done.

A replacement was found, and installed in my office. I gave her as much help as I could, and when my final day arrived, I left the office quietly, retrieved my car from the parking lot, and drove home through a snowstorm as tumultuous as my feelings. I felt as my daughter had felt when she boarded the British Airways flight to England. Have I made a big mistake?

The following morning dawned cold and bleak. At about ten o'clock the doorbell rang, and a smiling deliveryman said, "You must be pretty important. This is the largest bouquet I've ever delivered." Gorgeous long-stemmed spring flowers from John Powell filled two large crystal vases. I was just about to telephone him when he called to say that he had planned a special evening in Montreal for me, with all hundred-plus managers attending. A wonderful event took place at *Le Festin du Gouverneur* in the Old Fort, on Ste. Helene's Island. There were the usual speeches, and many gifts were presented. All were very much appreciated, and one in particular was just what the doctor ordered. Trans Canada presented me with two first-class round-trip tickets to anywhere on their system. The same stretch limo that had delivered me to Ste. Helene's Island waited until the last hurrah, and then delivered me home. I felt that my years in the industry had now really come to a close. It was nostalgic, but not sad. A whole new world would be opening for me. Thank you, John Powell. You're such a class act.

I had come a long way from the shy protected little girl who had so many times asked for a job at Colonial Airlines. What would have happened in my life had I not had a sister who by the grace of God happened to live on Peel Street above Sherbrooke? How about the only blind date I ever had? What are the chances that it would work out so well? I have been blessed so many times in so many ways.

FELLOW TRAVELLERS

Over the years, there have been many people in the travel industry whom I have admired. Some I knew from afar, others I worked with on a daily basis. Here are a few of those people with whom I shared the trials, tribulations, and joys of the ever- changing world of a life in the business we loved.

John Powell, past president of P. Lawson Travel and its affiliated companies (now Carlson Wagon-Lit). John was instrumental in building the company into the largest travel agency in Canada. While in university, his summer job was with P. Lawson Travel, and after graduation, he pursued a career in the industry he had grown to love. He founded the Alliance of Canadian Travel Agents (ACTA) at a time when such an association was sorely needed, as it is today. John was a good listener, had respect for all those with whom he came in contact, including personnel, service providers and competitors. With a great sense of humour, he could always see the funny side of a situation. He had the great ability to handle any problem with *savoir faire*. He is a gentleman, and a friend to many. He's a pretty good golfer too, even better now that he has more time to pursue his passion for the sport.

J. Boyce MacDougald, co-founder and past president of Voyages Bel-Air and senior vice-president of P. Lawson Travel and its affiliated companies (now Carlson Wagon-Lit). He was president of the Quebec division of the Alliance of Canadian Travel Agents. Boyce was known as "Mr. Travel," and was frequently consulted by airlines, suppliers and even competitors, for he was known to be fair and willing to lend a helping hand to others less knowledgeable or those in difficulty. He was a problem solver, a fine negotiator, a quick study, and was probably the brightest and most popular person in the industry. Montreal was saddened when he was called to Toronto. He returned many times to his favourite city, however, visiting his old friends and still making new ones. Although retired, he is still sought out by many in the industry for his wisdom and experience in travel related matters. His sense of humour is legendary, and his booming laughter is unmistakably "Boyce."

Gisèle Vinson. When Gisele applied for a position in Beaconsfield as a second career, her resumé read like a *Who's Who* in travel. She had worked for Pan American Airways, had started the Interline Club (a social club for Montreal airline employees) and had been voted by her peers as "The Most Popular Airline Employee in Montreal." Letters of recommendation were from several well-known and respected members of the industry. I felt lucky that she had chosen our agency as her first port of call. How fortunate I was, for Gisele became the best thing to happen to us. She was remarkably intelligent and had the ability to grasp a situation quickly, often saving the day with her logic. Clients migrated to her, and were always impressed with her knowledge and her interest in providing the perfect well-suited holiday. Still active in the travel sector, she is providing the kind of service that has always been her trademark.

Richard Copeman. Although I never worked side by side with Dick, I had occasion to speak with him several times a week, and on his frequent sales visits to our office. He was vice-president of Holiday House, a wholesale supplier of hotels, tours and ancillary services to travel agencies. In all of the years I dealt with Dick Copeman, he never once reneged on a promise, a commitment or agreement. These were always by handshake or by telephone. There are very few people about whom I can say this with certainty, and for that reason, Dick ranks very high on my list of responsible people. In the humour department, he ranks high as well.

Jacqueline Valois. One of the first people to join our team in Beaconsfield, Jackie was taking a correspondence course in travel when we spotted her, and asked her to be a part of our organization. Providing excellent service to our clientele, she worked diligently to make sure that each and every one would be pleased with her handling of travel arrangements. Jackie liked to visit the far corners of the earth, so that she could bring back stories of the various cultures to her travellers. She was an asset to us, and we were pleased that after about ten years with us she opened her own agency, which was a reward she deserved, and our loss. A sense of humour? You bet!

Jackie Munro. Jackie took a trip to the Rockies organized by our company, and liked it so much she applied for a part-time job with us. We agreed to train her, and in doing so, I found that her mind was so quick, I couldn't keep up with it. Being an avid and accurate note taker, she never once missed a deadline, nor was she ever late for an appointment. Her word was her bond and her reading of a situation was always fair and to the point. There came a time when family commitments required more of her time, and she left the travel business. Jackie was missed by everyone, staff and clientele alike. Fortunately, some years later, Jackie could give me some time, and acted as my secretary. Thank God for her sense of timing, keeping me on track! And yes, we had many laughs.

Lynne Castonguay Kirby. Lynn was able to work for us only part time, and what a pity that was for me. She was the person who took all new young employees under her wing, and gave them the nourishing I wish I had been able to give. She was the glue that kept all of the staff together, and even now little old ladies approach me in the shopping centre to tell me nice stories about Lynne's helping them plan their trip, her patience and her encouraging nature. She never saw herself as being important, but she was to me and to all who knew her. And yes, she was quick-witted, funny, able to turn catastrophic chaos into calm sailing. What an athlete she was as well – tennis and skiing were favourites. We were privileged to know you, Lynne. R.I.P

Harold J. Canvin, "Hank" to everyone. I met Hank in 1946 when he became my boss, as district sales manager of Northeast Airlines (later Delta Airlines). He resisted the opportunities he had to go south, becoming Delta's top executive in Canada. I always thought he should have moonlighted as a radio news anchor, for his voice was distinctive, with soft, soothing, well-modulated tones. I never saw Hank lose his cool, even under the most strenuous circumstances. He was dedicated to his beloved airline, and remains so until this day as he continues his career with Delta Airlines. As a councilman for the city of Kirkland, Hank helped to build that town. Having done such an outstanding job, the town named Canvin Street in his honour. He always respected the rights of others, and was a fair negotiator. Everyone who has ever dealt with Hank praises his sterling character, his knowledge and his depth of caring for others. Here's to you, Hank !

Donna Hughes. After a successful teaching career, Donna opted to change course and enter the travel field. She attended my first travel course at John Abbott College, after which she joined our staff in Beaconsfield for further training. Wishing to have control over the hours she worked, she decided to become an "outside representative" for us, bringing in new business. She also developed the market to Portugal, accompanying groups on a regular basis to Sesimbra, Portugal. She was a natural in the business. A fine researcher, she was able to capture the delights of any destination, ascertain the validity of claims by hotels and services and pass them on to prospective clientele. Her diplomacy was an asset to our company along with her ability to handle difficult assignments. Donna is still with the company, now known as Carlson Wagon-Lit, and is well respected in the world of travel.

Madeline Martin. A career as an executive secretary was a good background when Madeline decided to change gears and enter the travel industry. She was able to remember the most minute of details pertaining to any client, and related well to the inexperienced traveller as well as the frequent vacationer. Having just returned from several years in Africa, she took a travel course and then applied for a position with our office in Beaconsfield. Her experience in Africa was certainly an asset, for travel to that part of the world was just beginning to open up. Promoted to the position of manager in the Pointe-Claire office, Madeleine was instrumental in making it one of the most successful locations of the company. Her devotion to duty was an outstanding quality that I admired. She is still working wonders in the Pointe-Claire office, which is now Carlson Wagon-Lit.